The Retreat Leader's Manual

Our gift to you!

Helping you connect with God and each other!

We're here to help you with your next retreat!

info@sandycove.org
www.sandycove.org
800.234.COVE (2683)

The Retreat
Leader's Manual

A Complete Guide to
Organizing Meaningful Christian Retreats

NANCY FERGUSON AND KEVIN WITT

DISCIPLESHIP RESOURCES

P O BOX 340003 • NASHVILLE, TN 37203-0003
www.discipleshipresources.org

Cover design by Thelma Whitworth.
Interior design by PerfecType, Nashville, TN.

ISBN 13: 978-0-88177-428-3
ISBN 10: 0-88177-428-6

Library of Congress Control Number 2006937848

CONTENTS

Thanks to All Retreat Leaders

We want to begin by giving a big thanks to all of you who say, "Yes", to guiding retreats. We share your passion for partnering with God to nurture people's souls. Thousands upon thousands of people point to retreats as pivotal in their faith journeys. Without teams to plan and provide these opportunities, many would miss out on some of the most enriching faith formation experiences of their lives.

We know that a number of you step forward without much training, because it is not readily available in your local setting. Some of you take on this endeavor as part as your congregational staff responsibilities, while for others it flows from your desire to make a difference through volunteer service. Whether you are a veteran or launching out for the first time, we hope this manual will encourage and support you.

Preparing a retreat takes time and energy. Fortunately, is, also, very gratifying. We pray that you will be richly blessed through your willingness give this gift for others. Know that the Holy Spirit actively participates in the process, so the experience doesn't rest entirely on your shoulders. Wonderful things will happen. Lean on God and even difficulties that arise can be catalysts for joy, goodness and meaning.

Many thanks also go to those who were inspirational and supportive of us during the writing process. Special thanks go to those who shared their time and insights to read portions of this manuscript: Nancy Fitzgerald, Lisa van der Plogg, Bruce Harvey, Treva Sasser, Alice Blanton, Tim Holt Duncan, Diana Davidson, Cindy Ruhl, Pamela Mitchell-Legg, Will Evans, Marcey Balcomb, and Steve Coons.

We are convinced that today's church members are hungry for the rest, sense of belonging, and meaning that retreats provide. It is our prayer that this book will enable more and more people to have these experiences.

Nancy Ferguson
Richmond, Virginia

Kevin Witt
Bend, Oregon

INTRODUCTION

The weekend had been filled with laughter, conversation around the tables, sounds of children, small groups working together to plan skits and make banners, worship by the light of candles, and good food. The beautiful fall weather invited folks outside to walk through the crunch of leaves and to watch the reflections on the lake. On Friday evening the smell of the campfire filled the air as marshmallows were roasted in preparation for s'mores. The days began and ended with singing. Late on Saturday afternoon, retreat participants—all members of a small congregation—sat around the table for worship and to celebrate communion. "What did this experience mean to you?" the worship leader asked the people gathered there. One woman responded, "I have been a member of this church for over fifteen years, but in the last twenty-four hours I have learned more about the people in this community than I have learned in all the years before. There was time and space this weekend to talk together in a way we just don't have in the ordinary busyness of our lives."

This story is just one of the stories told by pastors, church leaders, and congregational members over the years about congregational retreat experiences. These accounts of church leaders clearly recognize the importance of retreat experiences in the faith formation of those who follow Jesus Christ. Retreats strengthen the ministry of the church, nurture the faith of believers, and deepen relationships.

A 2003 survey conducted by a mainline denomination asked pastors, church leaders, and laypeople about their formative faith experiences. Four in ten church members and the majority of pastors reported having a "significant spiritual experience" within a camp, retreat, or conference setting. The same survey found that 58% of congregations sponsored one or more retreats in the year prior to the survey.

Retreats are characterized by leaving behind the regular rush and demands of every-day work and family life to come to a place apart where encounters with God, with others in community, and creation are possible. These encounters put the emphasis on the interconnection and relatedness of all of life. Through retreat experiences, participants have the time and space to reflect on scripture, pray, enjoy the company of one another, and rejoice in the beauty of God's creation. The result of these times away is a renewal of faith and commitment to Jesus Christ.

The goal of this book is to equip you to plan and lead retreat experiences for members of your congregation. If you have never planned a retreat and thought you never could, then it is the hope of this book that you will be enabled to do that through the information and guidance provided here. On the other hand, if you are an experienced retreat leader, it is equally the hope of the book that you will find new ideas and insights for future retreat leadership.

The three sections of the book include both theoretical foundations and practical helps for retreat ministry. The biblical and theological section identifies the ways in which retreat experiences provide the opportunity for encounters with God, with others, and with creation. The practical sections include a collection of worship, study, and community activities, as well as a step-by-step process for planning a meaningful and effective retreat.

The Purpose of this Handbook

The book is directed toward the variety of people within congregations who want to learn more about planning retreats and who will take on the primary responsibility for the leading the retreat planning process. Perhaps you are a pastor or educator who has had significant retreat experiences and desire to pass this experience on to others; perhaps you have never gone on a retreat but have heard about the meaning it has had for others; perhaps you are a church educator charged with oversight of the church's annual retreat and are searching for new ideas. The book can meet the needs of each type of retreat leader.

All kinds of groups within a congregation who are planning a retreat will find this book useful, including youth, women's, or men's groups, church leaders, or special interest groups. The resource is written in such a way that all groups using the book will find the information they need. Many congregations have discovered the benefits and joys of a church family retreat in which all members of the congregation are invited to join together. Much of the planning process has in mind a church-wide retreat, but can be modified for other groups. Several suggestions specifically for youth retreats have been noted in the risk management section.

Structure of the Book

The book is divided into three major sections. Each of these sections contributes to the unique nature of this resource for the planning and leadership tasks of retreats.

Section one, written by Kevin Witt, offers congregational leaders an opportunity to delve more deeply into the scriptural and theological foundations of Christian retreat ministries. Use this section as a resource for reflection and study about the benefits and purpose of including retreats as part of the church's ministry. In addition, the material in the section can be used as background information in the development of retreat themes.

Section two, written by Nancy Ferguson, examines the opportunities for experiential and relational practices offered by the retreat setting. Organized around three types of encounters—with God, others, and creation—the section provides both a rationale for encounter practices and examples of activities for the encounters. It includes suggestions for worship, Bible study, community building, recreation, and hospitality. As a Retreat Planning Committee creates the retreat design, it can weave together the encounter practices into the whole retreat experience.

Section three, also written by Nancy Ferguson, focuses on the administrative tasks necessary to plan all aspects of the retreat, from setting the date to evaluating the event. Once congregational leaders identify the valuable contribution to the faith formation of believers that retreats can make, they can establish a Retreat Planning Committee to plan the retreat. That group can make good use of this book in designing and developing all aspects of the retreat.

This final section is all about the details, and provides step-by-step guidance for the each aspect of the planning process. It begins with ideas for gathering a Retreat Planning Team and a schedule for this team to use in its planning, as well as detailed information about choosing a retreat center, promoting the retreat, keeping participants safe, and evaluation.

Congregational leaders may use this resource at many points in the retreat planning process. The book provides an introduction of the benefits offered by retreats for the formation of faith and renewal of commitment to Christ. For this reason, leaders responsible for faith formation and nurture within a congregation will find food for thought and a jumping off place to begin planning for a retreat.

Many who use this book will be pastors or educators charged with oversight of educational and nurture ministries within a congregation. Many ministry staffs constantly seek to broaden their theological understanding and practical skills for all kinds of ministry. This resource is committed to equipping them for the task of leading retreats and working with Retreat Planning Committees, regardless of their experience level. All three sections of the book will enhance their knowledge and practice.

Others who use this resource will be lay volunteer leaders on the Retreat Planning Committee charged with seeing that the retreat actually happens from beginning to end. Their planning process will be enriched by a review of biblical foundations. They will want to become familiar with the encounter practices found in section two, and with the details of the planning process in section three.

Purpose of the Book

Although this resource addresses the biblical foundations for having retreats and the practical aspects of designing program and planning, the goal of the book is the enrichment of faith. It is during the silence and separateness of retreats that God's presence is known through solitude, times of worship, walks in the woods, over meals, and in quiet conversations. These encounters with God comfort, reassure, challenge, convert, reclaim, call, and inspire believers, leading them toward more faithful lives as disciples of Jesus Christ. The goal of this book is to provide a steady structure for God's encounters with God's people. The authors pray that this book will offer you opportunities for encounters with God through life in community within a natural setting for members of your congregation.

Section One:
Biblical and
Theological
Foundations

Pathways Offered by Christian Retreats

Many retreat books present a multitude of activity and theme ideas, but seem sadly starved of information on the biblical and theological foundations of Christian retreat ministry. It is a major advantage for retreat leaders to feast on the tantalizing breadth of theology, which nourishes the spirit of both the retreat guide and participants. Greater understanding of the nutrient rich retreat tradition brings a balance of offerings that will truly sustain.

This first section of the book is dedicated to those of you who want to go beyond simply skimming the surface. In large part, the difference between being a general activity leader and a retreat leader comes in knowing how to choose experiences that truly match the mission of retreats. It is the purpose of this first section of the book to delve more deeply into the principles and pathways that inform decisions about what will benefit and what will detract from the retreat experience.

Christian retreats have a special focus that goes beyond personal growth or typical vacation getaways. All church retreats have a spiritual dimension that recognizes the Spirit of God—the Holy Spirit. Retreats provide a period of withdrawal from disruption and unending responsibilities. They allow us to step out of the rut of routine, so we can look upon our lives and the world with God in mind.

Retreats might be defined this way: the choice to enter places and times apart from busyness and distraction, in order to develop deeper connections with God and a greater appreciation for life. That, in a nutshell, is the reason why the church over the centuries has so passionately pursued the establishment of the retreat experience and retreat centers. These excursions have unparalleled attributes that prove very effective.

A good return is actually part of the retreat, too. The goal is for participants to return home to continue applying the insights and practices gained. Every retreat continues through a creative homecoming that shapes new interactions and priorities of participants and affect their families, churches, communities, and the wider world. In a true sense, people regain a balance that allows for more abundant living. There are ways of knowing God and ourselves that exist only beyond nonstop motion and work.

It seems wise not to overcomplicate or to underestimate the central aim of this ministry, or we could easily drift to the periphery. There are hosts of organizations that offer a plethora of positive programs and attractions (and some not so positive programs and attractions), but there are very few beyond religious communities whose primary concern is to help people connect more deeply with God and to be in greater touch with the beauty and sacredness of life. This is something to value and cherish about our contribution and Christian identity.

We must be careful not to trade this for simply mimicking popular fads and amenities already easily available elsewhere. A higher hope moves us toward God, who offers more enduring joy and meaning, not just short-lived entertainment. How disappointing to participants if they come and find only a wisp of what they long for.

Prudent and fruitful selection of retreat components rests upon keeping constantly in mind what the experience is ultimately all about. For example, encouraging people to watch television in their own rooms does not contribute to spiritual growth or the purposes of the retreat. Sadly, this actually sends people back to what they already have and know, rather than expanding their awareness. This is but one example of the types of discernment you can consider thoroughly as you design the retreat.

The Paradox and Power of Retreats

Guiding retreats requires trust and faith because retreats are counter-intuitive to so many messages of mainstream consumer culture that seem to have soaked into our very pores. It will likely take encouragement, confidence, and positive support from you to motivate participants to welcome the seeming paradoxes of faith. Some of the unexpected invitations retreats offer are include: receiving through letting go, moving closer by being still, hearing through silence, advancing by retreat, acting on God's behalf by resting, learning community from solitude and strangers, going away to become more present, finding abundance in producing less, embracing yourself by reaching out, listening to the language of nature, leading by being a servant of all, honoring diversity through simplicity, and loving your enemies.

Retreat experiences, these "places apart to be together", welcome persons into what long time camp and retreat leader, Ted Witt, calls "a change of pace, place, and face."

In other words, participants enter an alternative cadence of living, while venturing to less familiar surroundings and leaving behind many roles that give them a sense of predictability and comfort. That is fantastic! Be sensitive and caring, however, while simultaneously stimulating chances for positive transformations within the newness and nuances inherent in journeying away.

Retreat experiences ask folks to launch from their harbors into the unknown that characterizes any adventure. All this produces powerful potential. As people move through their initial uncertainty, it opens a host of new horizons. Biblical stories are full of persons who encountered God or gained greatly expanded awareness through new situations and excursions. You are part of offering the opportunity!

Three Primary Pathways

Over the centuries, Christian leaders have discovered avenues that often open people to new encounters with God, with others, and with the creation. Christian retreats built on solid biblical and theological foundations can be a true reflection of Christ's life and teachings. This manual is organized around three retreat routes and the practices they suggest. We hope you enjoy diving a little deeper to explore these three types of encounters that retreats offer, which help us experience dimensions of the grace and love of God. These are:

1. Encounters with God
2. Encounters with Others within Community
3. Encounters with the Creation

In the following chapters, the biblical and theological foundations of each encounter will be explored in greater depth. For each "Encounter" there will be a broad look at the theological and faith issues accompanied by a closer look at several pertinent scripture passages. Later in the program section of the book, the suggested practices will relate directly to the biblical and theological understandings developed here.

Encounters
with God

Periods of rest, renewal, silence and solitude have long been characteristic of faith-based retreats, with very good reason. Today, we live in an era when never-ending motion and activity rank high as signs of cutting edge productivity to be admired. This is true at one level, but a half-truth.

Many travelers on retreat arrive heavily burdened. Jesus promises rest for their souls (Matthew 11:28-29). Rest, renewal, and play are precious pathways we provide, especially for these individuals. If we align ourselves with Christ's promise, they can access an avenue for Christ to fulfill that promise. Retreats become the occasion to learn how to allow God to nurture our souls. Ultimately, retreats encourage people to return with new perspective and practices to incorporate within their weekly and daily rhythms. For in the end, Augustine reminds us in his well-known maxim, "Thou hast made us for thyself, O Lord, and our hearts are restless until they find their rest in thee."[1] By their very nature, retreats are temporary, but the way of life is not.

Welcome to the spiritual frontier that offers a broader perspective on existence. In the words of Robert Frost, you will be engaging participants in a "road less traveled" that "has made all the difference" for millions who seek God. Retreats draw persons to settings and rhythms often unfamiliar for citizens of the frenzy we call modern life. For most people, the constant message in their daily lives is if you are not "doing" or "producing" something, then it is a complete waste of time. Alas, even children's play has become a highly organized, pressure packed project in so many cases.

This is not to dismiss the benefits of effort, labor, and doing good works. As James says:

> What good is it, my brothers and sisters, if you say you have faith but do not have works? Can faith save you? If a brother or sister is naked and lacks daily food, and one of you says to them, "Go in peace; keep warm and eat your fill," and yet you do not supply their bodily needs, what is the good of that? So faith by itself, if it has no works, is dead. But someone will say, "You have faith and I have works." Show me your faith apart from your works, and I by my works will show you my faith (James 2:14-18).

Even though faith produces good works, faith does not equate to unceasing doing and accomplishments. Faith is, at its core, trust in and love for God. Great acts of faithfulness call us to respites, renewal, worship, and solitude, Biblical reading and reflection, prayer, and silence express that love and trust. Our lives can quickly lose their equilibrium and joy without this balance.

An often unexpressed fear is that it will be terribly boring, if the group or individuals are not constantly entertained by highly active pursuits while on retreat. Without TV screens to look at, without constant sound and conversation, and without the type of interactions give definition to how people see themselves, who will they be and what will they do? All this can be intimidating. For some, it will be a welcomed reprieve, but others will hesitate. The enthusiasm and confidence of the retreat leader does much to allay these concerns. You will need to be a teacher of new practices, as well as an advocate for them.

Margaret Silf sheds light on the strengths of stepping away in her book, *Going on Retreat*. A retreat is not a retreat from real life, but rather a retreat toward real life.

> . . . I remain convinced that when we go deep into the heart of ourselves, we also come closer to the heart of each other—therefore a retreat is not a retreat from others but a retreat to what is at the heart of all life . . . to make a retreat is not to escape from the real world, but to be in touch with aspects of reality that are often covered up by distractions and busyness . . . Things are the other way around: we are often escaping from reality (what is truly important and life giving) when we are so busy doing . . . , and we are facing and encountering a deeper reality when we take time to be still and to listen to the movements of our hearts.[2]

Shortly before his tragic death in an auto accident, Mike Yaconelli, the co-founder of Youth Specialties (a highly regarded provider of training and resources for adult workers with youth), expressed his alarm regarding the direction many Christian camp and retreat ministries seem to be drifting. One of the last insights Mike passed on to colleagues appears as an article in the *Journal of Christian Camping* entitled, "Is this Christian Camping (Retreating)?" Here are some poignant excerpts:

I spoke recently at a family conference held at a resort-like retreat center on a lake. The setting was beautiful: a pristine lake, lofty pine trees, hundreds of trails, sandy beaches, flowers and views too numerous to mention. Talk about a place where you could get away from the hectic pace . . . Talk about opportunities to be alone with God. Not a chance . . . I was shocked by the schedule. Beginning at 6:30 in the morning and ending at midnight; the schedule was crammed with every activity imaginable . . . The first evening, I noticed the fatigue on the faces of the adults and youth . . . These people made a decision to retreat . . . the exact opposite happened. Here's the sad part; the people at the conference loved it . . . (They weren't aware of what they were missing). This was not a retreat. It was an extension of the way of life they were already leading back home.[3]

Scriptural and Theological Exploration for Retreat Leaders

Within the Judeo-Christian tradition, we find a stimulating stream of passages that highlight the beauty and benefits of Sabbath, solitude and silence. Read carefully, for these messages form a well of blessing that retreat leaders and participants have drawn upon for generations to guide them.

Provide Opportunities for Participants to Quench Their Thirst for God

> As a deer longs for flowing streams, so my soul longs for you, O God. My soul thirsts for God, for the living God. When shall I come and behold the face of God? (Psalm 42:1-2).

> For surely I know the plans I have for you, says the LORD, plans for your welfare and not for harm, to give you a future with hope. Then when you call upon me and come and pray to me, I will hear you. When you search for me, you will find me; if you seek me with all your heart (Jeremiah 29:11-13).

Spiritual retreats tap into a universal human desire. Sometimes it is hard for people to articulate, but we all long to connect more deeply with God. Retreats tap into a widespread search in modern society that some cannot fully articulate, but which has sparked their interest in spirituality. Retreats serve as an oasis for the soul where people can drink of the "living water". Retreats are about removing the barriers that keep people from noticing and relating with the ever-present Love, who is with us and for us. The unabashed aim of faith-based retreats is helping persons seek God with their whole heart.

Stimulate Sacred Sabbath Time

> Remember the Sabbath day, and keep it holy. Six days you shall labor and do all your work. But the seventh day is a Sabbath to the LORD your God; you shall not do any work . . . For in six days the LORD made heaven and earth, the sea, and all that is in them, but rested the seventh day; therefore the LORD blessed the Sabbath day and consecrated it (Exodus 20:8-11).

> "Come to me, all you that are weary and are carrying heavy burdens, and I will give you rest. Take my yoke upon you, and learn from me; for I am gentle and humble in heart, and you will find rest for your souls" (Matthew 11: 28-29).

It is fascinating how much of an emphasis the scriptures place on Sabbath time, unequivocally declaring it holy. The sacred circle includes ceasing from creating, abstaining from advancing and braving a break, in order to enjoy the present. Our lives can pass us by while we are striving for the future. It is not about "doing nothing." Rather, laying aside the rigors of routine represents a proactive passage toward God. Renewal and enjoyment of life are a natural outcome, but thanksgiving and worship is the main current. This high habit of Sabbath not only derives from Divine instruction, it is linked to the launching of life itself. (See Genesis 1:31-2:3.)

Reality resounds in these teachings. The fullness of life never proceeds from packing it completely with unending goals and tasks. Emptying ourselves and our schedules on a regular basis expands our existence rather than diminishing it. This ebb and flow that alternates accomplishment with harkening our hearts to God is vital to our physical, emotional and spiritual well-being.

Perhaps Jewish leaders best explain this tradition, because they have been practicing it for centuries. It is from Jewish roots that this weekly faith holiday became a Christian spiritual practice as well. Sabbath is about the fitting culmination of effort and blessing, enjoyment and thanksgiving. *What Christians Should Know about Jews and Judaism* written by Rabbi Yechiel Eckstein offers insights that help us avoid misinterpretation of Sabbath. Here are three quotes to ponder:

> Of all the holidays in the Jewish year, the weekly Sabbath is the most cherished and beloved . . . It's depth might be summed up in the words of the Psalmist "O to taste and see that the Lord is good.[4]

While the Shabbat (Sabbath) has been universally acclaimed, it has also, unfortunately, often been grossly misunderstood. It is commonly believed that the Shabbat is observed in order to replenish our physical strength and to enable us to work energetically and productively during the coming week . . . (Keep in mind, however, that) it is not the beginning of the week, but the culmination of the week and zenith of living not simply a preparation for living . . . The Jew's entire week is lived in anticipation of the Shabbat. Everything points to it; everything leads to it. And while it is certainly true that the Shabbat rejuvenates, replenishes and revitalizes so that we are able to face another work week, the deeper meaning of the Shabbat is that it is observed not for the sake of the rest of the week, but that the rest of the week is the prologue for the arrival of Shabbat.[5]

True freedom is freedom from servitude to human goals in order to know and serve God . . . For this reason the Torah states, "Thou shalt not do any work—you, your sons, daughters, slaves, animals and strangers in your midst" (Exodus 20:10). Everyone and everything is to be free on this day, in order that they might embrace something more ultimate in their lives . . . Humanity can become his/her own taskmaster when enslaving oneself to non-ultimates that bring no tranquility to mind, body and soul...Moses expressed this same concept of freedom when he pleaded with Pharaoh in the name of God to "let my people go so they may worship me' (Exodus 8:20)."[6]

Taking repeated hiatus to appreciate the present, triggers thankfulness. Noticing the blessings begins with gifts so simple and central as consciousness of the breaths we breathe, which supply and sustain us thousands of times per day. What better way to say thanks than to have enough faith to let go and just be—to glorify God rather than piling on the pressure to be God?

Self-care and renewal recognizes the preciousness of the Spirit with and within us. Part of the Sabbath tradition lifts up freedom from slavery that is a vital theme within the story of the people of God. God freed us from slavery, and we are not to return to the slavery of never ending labor even if it is self-imposed. Rest is righteous, too. It is a way to serve God and honor God. Abraham Heschel, expresses it this way. "Just to be is a blessing. Just to live is holy."[7]

What a difference it makes in our families, our communities, and our planet, when we habitually pause from producing and consuming in order to truly experience the daily miracles that exist all around us. Perhaps this was part of what Jesus was trying to say to

Martha when he refused to affirm Martha's request for her sister Mary to trade time with Christ in favor of labor (Luke 10:38-42).

Introduce Silence and Stillness as Sources for Sensing God

> He said, "Go out and stand on the mountain before the LORD, for the LORD is about to pass by." Now there was a great wind, so strong that it was splitting mountains and breaking rocks in pieces before the LORD, but the LORD was not in the wind; and after the wind an earthquake, but the LORD was not in the earthquake; and after the earthquake a fire, but the LORD was not in the fire; and after the fire a sound of sheer silence. When Elijah heard it, he wrapped his face in his mantle and went out and stood at the entrance of the cave. Then there came a voice to him that said, "What are you doing here, Elijah?" (1 Kings 19:11-13).

> "Be still, and know that I am God!" (Psalm 46:10).

There is so much static, noise and commotion in the modern milieu. Silence and stillness are like precious jewels, because of their rarity. These pathways can be remarkably powerful modes to getting in touch with the Holy Spirit and what is truly important in life. Teach people to welcome silence and stillness as a proactive step to greater awareness, rather than simply a lull in the action.

Invite Participants into Periods of Prayer and Solitude

> In the morning, while it was still very dark, he got up and went out to a deserted place, and there he prayed (Mark 1:35).

> The apostles gathered around Jesus, and told him all that they had done and taught. He said to them, "Come away to a deserted place all by yourselves and rest a while." For many were coming and going, and they had no leisure even to eat (Mark 6:30).

Solitude has an amazing way of promoting presence, even though it might appear contrary to the undiscerning eye. Jesus, as hectic as his ministry could sometimes be, purposely sought out solitude to renew his relationship with God and to support his soul. Solitude is not loneliness or being alone, as much as it is being with God and being with oneself. These encounters often enable persons to better embrace others, also, when they return.

We should not underrate the infusion of seclusion for spiritual growth. These occasions often bring one face to face with the big questions of life. This includes reflection about our direction and purpose. Jesus' own life has numerous illustrations. He followed the guidance of the Holy Spirit into the wilderness right after his baptism and affirmation from God. There he wrestled with what priorities would guide him (Matthew 3:16- 4:11). He ventured alone to the mountains to pray, and then returned ready to recruit his disciples and launch the next phase of his ministry (Luke 6:12-13). Jesus journeyed to the garden of Gethsemane and, a short distance from his followers, met alone with God where he contemplated the most crucial and painful period he would face (Luke 22:39-33). Seeking solitude was a holy habit for Jesus.

Notes

1. Saint Augustine, *The Confessions of Saint Augustine*, translated by Edward Pusey (New York: P.F. Collier and Son, 1909-14 Volume 7, Part 1 of 51 in the series Harvard Classics), quote listed on http://www.bartleby.com/7/1/1.html.

2. Margaret Silf, *Going on Retreat*, (Chicago: Loyola Press, 2002), 19.

3. Mike Yaconelli, *Is this Christian Camping?* (Colorado Springs, CO: Christian Camping and Conference Journal, July/August 2003,), 11-12.

4. Rabbi Yechiel Eckstein, *What Christians Should know about Jews and Judaism*, (Waco Texas: Word Books,1984), 81.

5. Eckstein, 83.

6. Eckstein, 88.

7. Kirk Byron Jones, *Addicted to Hurry: Spiritual Strategies for Slowing Down*, (Valley Forge, PA: Judson Press, 2003), 45.

Encounters
with Others

We live in a time when people long for connections, but often hesitate to reach out to form new relationships. Families move from place to place more often today than in previous generations, thus displacing them from tight knit family and friends. Individuals frequently do not even know their own neighbors. Even members of the same congregation may know each other only on a superficial level. Moving from discomfort and, at times, general suspicion of strangers to friendship is a precious blessing highly valued within the Christian retreat setting. Inspiring persons to truly welcome each other and to form a community of belonging gives them an opportunity to give and receive love, which enriches all their lives.

What is commonly referred to as "community" in general parlance falls far short of fulfilling the yearning of the heart. Definitions of community run the spectrum, from simply being in a homogenous group who think alike, to a collection of homes in the same housing development. Genuine love, however, expands the meaning of community by drawing people together despite their differences. The movement from mere politeness and tolerance to a greater level of care and interaction emerges when a group opens themselves to the Spirit of God. Christ models for us a wide embrace, including those shunned by others.

In his book, *The Road Less Traveled*, M. Scott Peck defines the love that births true community as:

> The will to extend one's self for the purpose of nurturing one's own or another's spiritual growth.[1]

This description deserves serious reflection. First, community requires that we decide to extend ourselves. It is not just a feeling of good intentions. In fact, love can occur even if we don't necessarily feel like it or can't affirm everything about another person. It is a deliberate choice to go beyond fears and barriers. It is the will and self-discipline to put forth energy to reach out to the other, beyond normal distinctions and separations, as a way to honor and support God's presence with and within them.

Such a heartfelt practice requires sensitivity and attentiveness. Only by actually listening, in order to better understand and appreciate one another more, can we recognize what will truly build each other up. Getting to know each other by name is just the beginning. Community comes alive through love determined to act on behalf of the other. This means that we do all we are able to create environments of hospitality that invite people to seek God as well as value and uplift one another.

It is our privilege and our calling, as retreat leaders and planners, to encourage people to love one another, but it is not always simple and easy. We, ourselves, will have many opportunities to allow God to shape us to become more loving through the real life situations that arise when we host folks on retreat. Christian retreats invite both the leaders and the participants to open themselves to positive transformations drawn from God's guidance and the Holy Spirit's encouragement.

A dedication to this level of love and community helps reveal and screen out other motives that sometimes look deceptively like love, but really aren't. Some common reasons for extending oneself are: wanting to look good in the eyes of others, wanting to satisfy our own insecurities, trying to fix the other person and make them more like us, feeling compelled by guilt or the need to please, wanting to benefit the person so he or she will do the same in return, "doing our job" so the retreat will be deemed successful and people will come again, etc. Motive matters. Sincere community has the potential to occur when we truly have an abiding interest in each other's welfare that reflects God's abiding love.

Courage and faith definitely come into play to overcome the resistance and lethargy that sometimes hold us back. Community cannot exist without honesty, which may include saying the truth in love in ways that will be truly beneficial. These can be difficult but powerful encounters after people grow to appreciate and trust one another. What is best for one's soul at times calls for us to grow in love. Depth of mutual care and the beauty of true friendship produce some of the most joyous experiences of people's lives. Remember, however, that community ultimately comes as a gift of the Spirit. It is not simply something that can be manufactured and guaranteed for every group.

In her book, *Catholic America: Self-renewal Centers and Retreats*, Patricia Christian-Mayer quotes Abbot David Geraets on the importance of this aspect of the retreat experience.

"The best way to communicate a religious experience is in a loving community. Human love is probably the best medium to communicate the Holy Spirit. So people come into our community and they sort of 'catch' the Spirit, they 'catch' prayer, they 'catch' Christianity more than having it taught to them." [2]

Scriptural and Theological Exploration for Retreat Leaders

Holy Hospitality: Welcome the Stranger

For the LORD your God is God of gods and Lord of lords, the great God, mighty and awesome, who is not partial and takes no bribe, who executes justice for the orphan and the widow, and who loves the strangers, providing them food and clothing. You shall also love the stranger, for you were strangers in the land of Egypt (Deuteronomy 10:17-19).

"Then the king will say to those at his right hand, 'Come, you that are blessed by my Father, inherit the kingdom prepared for you from the foundation of the world; for I was hungry and you gave me food, I was thirsty and you gave me something to drink, I was a stranger and you welcomed me, I was naked and you gave me clothing, I was sick and you took care of me, I was in prison and you visited me.' Then the righteous will answer him, 'Lord, when was it that we saw you hungry and gave you food, or thirsty and gave you something to drink? And when was it that we saw you a stranger and welcomed you, or naked and gave you clothing? And when was it that we saw you sick or in prison and visited you?' And the king will answer them, 'Truly I tell you, just as you did it to one of the least of these who are members of my family, you did it to me'" (Matthew 25: 34-40).

Let mutual love continue. Do not neglect to show hospitality to strangers, for by doing that some have entertained angels without knowing it (Hebrews 13:1-2).

When a newcomer resides with you in your land, you shall not oppress the newcomer. The alien who resides with you shall be to you as the citizen among you; you shall love the alien as yourself, for you were aliens in the land of Egypt: I am the LORD your God (Leviticus 19:33-34).

Frequently, retreats bring people together who are strangers to us and to one another. Some people we will have literally never met before. Even people who attend the same congregation often arrive with little familiarity of one another beyond surface introductions. They may not even know each other's names. Christian retreats are sacred times of living in temporary Christian community twenty-four hours per day together. They are meaningful opportunities for strangers to become friends. This process takes time and happens through shared experiences and reflection by the group. Retreats provide magnificent and sometimes rare chances to join with people from different backgrounds, religions, races, and nationalities, in the love of Christ.

Your own welcome of strangers and inspiring them to welcome each other are faith filled acts, because they embody God's love of the stranger. The Judeo-Christian heritage holds this as a premier value. Providing hospitality includes an inherent humility as well, which acknowledges that we are often in the position of being a stranger ourselves and it is part of the story of the people of God.

The host is not the only one who gives. The stranger or guest often turns out to be the giver from God and the host the recipient. Check out just a few of the biblical encounters, when an act of hospitality leads to a revelation from God. (See Genesis 18:1-14, Luke 24:28-32, Luke 19:1-10.)

The following quote from Henri Nouwen, in his book *Reaching Out*, unveils the depth and breadth of the practice of hospitality.

> . . . reaching out to our innermost being can lead to a reaching out to the many strangers whom we meet on our way through life. In our world full of strangers, estranged from their own past, culture and country, from their neighbors, friends and family, from their deepest self and their God, we witness a painful search for a hospitable place where life can be lived without fear and where community can be found. Although many, we might even say most, strangers in this world become easily the victim of a fearful hostility, it is possible for men and women and obligatory for Christians to offer an open and hospitable space where strangers can cast off their strangeness and become our fellow human beings. The movement from hostility to hospitality is hard and full of difficulties. Our society seems to be increasingly full of fearful, defensive, aggressive people anxiously clinging to their property and inclined to look at their surrounding world with suspicion, always expecting an enemy to suddenly appear, intrude and do harm. But still – that is our vocation: to convert the *hostis* into *hospes*, the enemy into a guest and to create the free and fearless space where brotherhood and sisterhood can be formed and fully experienced.[3]

Covenant to Love One Another and to Share the Fruit of the Spirit:

> Jesus answered, "The first is, 'Hear, O Israel: the Lord our God, the Lord is one; you shall love the Lord your God with all your heart, and with all your soul, and with all your mind, and with all your strength.' The second is this, 'You shall love your neighbor as yourself.' There is no other commandment greater than these" (Mark 12:29-31).

> There is no fear in love, but perfect love casts out fear; for fear has to do with punishment, and whoever fears has not reached perfection in love. We love because he first loved us. Those who say, "I love God," and hate their brothers or sisters, are liars; for those who do not love a brother or sister whom they have seen, cannot love God whom they have not seen. The commandment we have from him is this: those who love God must love their brothers and sisters also (1 John 4: 18-21).

> By contrast, the fruit of the Spirit is love, joy, peace, patience, kindness, generosity, faithfulness, gentleness, and self-control. There is no law against such things . . . If we live by the Spirit, let us also be guided by the Spirit (Galatians 5: 22-23, 25).

A proactive step in planting the realization that participants help create the experience they seek is to discuss what they need and hope for from one another and the retreat. Doing this up front in a natural, relaxed way allows people to listen and understand each other's expectations. These honest conversations about loving and caring for one another best occur early in the retreat after they have gotten to know each other initially. Introducing the above texts serves as one possible way to launch the topic of what love looks like. 1 Corinthians 13 is another profound reflection on love. These passages become a catalyst for pondering and dialogue about the kind of behaviors and interactions that will truly nurture each other. The group can create a brief covenant (promise to each other and God) in their own words. It can begin something like this: "We promise to love and care for each other by . . ."

Live Out Principles Given to the Early Church

> Let love be genuine; hate what is evil, hold fast to what is good; love one another with mutual affection; outdo one another in showing honor. Do not lag in zeal, be ardent in spirit, serve the Lord. Rejoice in hope, be

patient in suffering, persevere in prayer. Contribute to the needs of the saints; extend hospitality to strangers. Bless those who persecute you; bless and do not curse them. Rejoice with those who rejoice, weep with those who weep. Live in harmony with one another; do not be haughty, but associate with the lowly; do not claim to be wiser than you are. Do not repay anyone evil for evil, but take thought for what is noble in the sight of all. If it is possible, so far as it depends on you, live peaceably with all . . . Do not be overcome by evil, but overcome evil with good (Romans 12:9-17).

Above all, maintain constant love for one another, for love covers a multitude of sins. Be hospitable to one another without complaining. Like good stewards of the manifold grace of God, serve one another with whatever gift each of you has received. Whoever speaks must do so as one speaking the very words of God; whoever serves must do so with the strength that God supplies, so that God may be glorified in all things through Jesus Christ. To God belong the glory and the power forever and ever. Amen (1 Peter 4:8-11).

As God's chosen ones, holy and beloved, clothe yourselves with compassion, kindness, humility, meekness, and patience. Bear with one another and, if anyone has a complaint against another, forgive each other; just as the Lord has forgiven you, so you also must forgive. Above all, clothe yourselves with love, which binds everything together in perfect harmony. And let the peace of Christ rule in your hearts, to which indeed you were called in the one body. And be thankful (Colossians 3:12-15).

Forming a caring community does not mean that we will always be perfect at it. From time to time, situations urge us to step back and examine what is happening, then to decide how to respond so we can get back on track. These reminders to the early church remain as applicable today as ever. As retreat leaders, it is important to seek God and to open ourselves to be shaped in ways that we hope the retreat will produce for others.

Provide Opportunities to Contribute to the Common Good

Now there are varieties of gifts, but the same Spirit; and there are varieties of services, but the same Lord; and there are varieties of activities, but it is the same God who activates all of them in everyone. To each is given the manifestation of the Spirit for the common good (1 Corinthians 12:4-7).

Ultimately, for a person to feel truly a part of the retreat community it is important to appreciate the gifts they bring both through their ways of being and their abilities. Sincere recognition and thankfulness for the contributions every person makes to the whole experience honors the manifestation of the Spirit within him or her. Christian hospitality is a little different in this perspective. We not only graciously host our guests, but we invite them to contribute to the common good of each other. This is an important distinction that makes a Christian Camp and Retreat Center or experience different from staying at a typical hotel, for example. We may invite our guests and participants to help each other and to interact through a variety of services they do on behalf of the whole. We know this is part of building and becoming a community of faith, which other venues don't always emphasize in their modes of hospitality.

Notes

1. M. Scott Peck, *The Road Less Traveled*, (New York: Touchstone Book Simon and Schuster, 1978), 81.

2. Patricia Christian-Mayer, *Self-renewal Centers and Retreats*, (Santa Fe NM: John Muir Publications, 1989), 27.

3. Henri J. M. Nouwen, *Reaching Out*, (New York: Image Books Doubleday, 1975), 65 -66.

Encounters
with Creation

Have you ever noticed that the vast majority of Christian camp and retreat centers are located within, or adjacent to, natural surroundings? Where civilization has encroached, some centers resort to gardens or other avenues to assure that nature remains. This is no accident. Of course, such environments are beautiful and frequently peaceful. The intentional choice to incorporate nature into Christian retreat experiences goes far beyond that, however.

There is an unparalleled spiritual benefit to being outdoors. The creation opens people to God in special ways and often elicits joy. Faith communities have discovered time and time again that the natural world assists individuals to sense the presence of the Divine. Nature renews, stirs a sense of awe, and sparks thanksgiving to God that enriches the lives of retreat goers long after the retreat is over. Such encounters, and the consistent stories from those affected by these sacred times and spaces, have moved faith communities for centuries to cherish retreat experiences.

As Christians, we are among those who recognize that the natural world, in all its diversity, is beloved. God's love extends to the whole created community of life. In a time when the human impact on the natural world reaches levels heretofore unimaginable in the history of our planet, it is crucial for the church to step up boldly to teach society the inherent value of other creatures and ecosystems. It is also poignantly relevant in our own time to reclaim and re-emphasize teachings that have sometimes been forgotten or ignored. In God's design, creation nurtures Christian discipleship and care for the earth becomes one of the ways Christian discipleship expresses itself as love for everything that

God has made. Christian retreat settings give people close-up opportunities to appreciate and learn to care for the natural world.

The parable of the Good Samaritan is an example of love and discipleship that focuses on helping one who is hurting and in need. In modern times, the natural world might well be seen as one abused and left desolate. We must be cognizant that the choice is not between loving human beings or loving the rest of creation. We are called to love both. Advocates of true social and environmental justice are allies.

The same forces, attitudes, and choices that cause damage to people also cause damage to the environment. In fact, the people who suffer most from environmental degradation are overwhelmingly the poor and marginalized. What we do and how we choose to live has the potential to heal or to harm. Let us take up the spiritual practices of doing good and avoiding harm as part of Christian retreats, which takes into account the unique location of camp and retreat centers for this dimension of faith formation. People can take home the encounters and lessons from these settings to apply in their everyday lives, in the local church, and in the wider world. All this draws us closer to God, the maker and sustainer of life.

Scripture and Christian tradition depict creation as a process that births a community, not just human beings in isolation. Although there is not room here to print all the verses of Genesis 1-2 and Psalm 8, you are encouraged to read these accounts. In Genesis 1, each aspect of creation is declared to be good by God, even before human beings come on the scene. In this first creation account, humans actually share the "day" of creation with other land animals. In Genesis 2, human connection with the earth and the rest of creation gets expressed in the fact that we are "made from the dust of the earth". The word for earth or ground is "*Adamah*" in Hebrew, thus "Adam", which represents human, or "of the earth or ground". All life as we know it shares the same basic building blocks. We are a part of each other both theologically, and as it turns out, biologically.

We frequently have a tendency to try to set ourselves apart from nature and the rest of creation. We limit the stories of God's creation and God's love by assuming the story is ours alone. Too often, the rest of creation is treated simply as a backdrop or stage for the human drama. The universe, however, does not revolve around humanity, but instead centers in God who chose to launch a diverse interdependent community of life. One powerful way that congregations can reinforce this aspect of our faith is through camp and retreat experiences.

Human beings are given special characteristics and roles within the whole that in some real ways give us "dominion" (Genesis 1:26), but any sense of dominion must be derived from our identity as ones made in the "image of God". Our self-understanding and role is based on whom we understand God to be and God's loving desire for the whole creation. Nowhere does scripture declare that only human beings matter, or that we can separate ourselves from the rest of what is in the heart of God.

The following quote from the prominent teacher and evangelist, John Wesley, who helped launch the Methodist movement in Eighteenth Century England, provides but one example of Christian theologians affirming God's presence with the whole creation.

> The great lesson that our blessed Lord inculcates here . . . is that God is in all things, and that we are to see the Creator in the glass of every creature; that we should use and look upon nothing as separate from God . . . but with a true magnificence of thought survey heaven and earth and all that is therein as contained by God in the hollow of his hand, who by his intimate presence holds them all in being, who pervades and activates the whole created frame, and is in a true sense the soul of the universe.[1]

The priorities and practices of modern society destroy other creatures and habitat necessary for their survival at a rate unparalleled since human beings came on the scene. Sadly, Christians often participate in these destructive practices as well. This makes it particularly poignant and critical that our faith practices include embracing creation as part of our embrace with God. What wisdom and benefits from God are we obliterating because of our lack of care? Faith and biological issues intersect in the loving and life giving intentions of God. A powerful, positive role for people of faith is to urge our congregational members and the society at large to consider the degree to which other creatures and wilderness speak to us and support our spiritual growth and welfare. Our sensitivity to their welfare and sustainability grows from honoring our Creator and honoring life.

In many places today, the land and its creatures are being stressed non-stop, to the point that their own ability to recover is being undermined. We are working some species and the fertility of the land (and waters) to death. This type of enslavement runs counter to the overall guidance we have received about God's will and desires. Not only are we working non-stop ourselves (to our own detriment) we are requiring the same across much of the planet in order to fuel our seemingly unending appetite for more production and consumption. There is so much we can do to change the way we relate. We can choose to shift our priorities and begin to respect God's covenant with the land. We can be a nurturing force to help bring shalom—the peace and wholeness that God envisions. In so doing, we discover a greater wholeness within ourselves.

This is where social and ecological justice converge, because the same attitudes and priorities that oppress the poor also enslave the creation. The highly respected Christian theologian from Latin America, Leonardo Boff, describes it this way.

Liberation theology and ecological discourse have something in common; they start from two bleeding wounds. The wound of poverty breaks the social fabric of millions and millions of poor people around the world. The other wound, systematic assault on the Earth, breaks down the balance of the planet, which is under threat from the plundering of development as practiced by contemporary global societies. Both lines of reflection and practice have as their starting point a cry: the cry of the poor for life, freedom and beauty (cf. Ex. 3:7), and the cry of the Earth groaning under oppression (cf. Rom 8:22-23). Both seek liberation . . . [2]

God's immanent presence holds all creation in being. The whole creation speaks of God. The retreat experience offers a wonderful opportunity to remind participants to "look upon nothing as separate from God." The greatest commandment of our Christian faith—to love God, to love our neighbor, and to love ourselves—takes on new breadth. This recognition can shape the practices, programs, and lifestyles lifted up in retreat settings for application everywhere we journey and live.

Exploration of Scripture

The Creation Speaks of God

The heavens are telling the glory of God; and the firmament proclaims God's handiwork. Day to day pours forth speech, and night to night declares knowledge. There is no speech, nor are there words; their voice is not heard; yet their voice goes out through all the earth, and their words to the end of the world (Psalm 19: 1-4).

The scriptures give us insight into how connections with nature can play an important role in Christian spiritual growth. Here, the psalmist highlights an inherent feature of nature, if we have the ears to hear it. The creation is constantly telling the glory of God. Part of the retreat experience purpose is to invite persons outdoors, where participants can become a part of, observe, and "listen" to the voice of nature, which has its own language and way of communicating. Attentiveness encourages giving thanks and glorifying God in response. Nature aids those desiring to know and sense God's presence.

In the beginning was the Word, and the Word was with God, and the Word was God. He was in the beginning with God. All things came into being through him, and without him not one thing came into being. What has come into being in him was life, and the life was the light of all people. The light shines in the darkness, and the darkness did not over-come it . . . And the Word became flesh and lived among us, and we have seen his glory, the glory as of a father's only son, full of grace and truth (John 1:1-5, 14).

The writer of John makes an inseparable link between Christ and all of creation. All things come into being through the Word—the life-giving, creative source of the universe as we know it. The Word, which was with God and was God, communicates, in part, by birthing the whole process of creation into existence. The Gospel writer shares the good news that the same Word lived among us in Jesus, whose continual presence abides with us now. The natural world, then, is an expression, communication, and reflection of its Creator. The cosmos flows from God who brings forth the universe in connection with the Christ. All this life is a light from God.

As the Fourteenth Century Christian teacher, Meister Eckhart, said so well:

> Every single creature is full of God and is a book about God. Every crea-ture is a word of God. If I spent enough time with the tiniest creature— even a caterpillar—I would never have to prepare a sermon. So full of God is every creature [Meister Eckhart (1260-1329)]. [3]

What God brings into being, therefore, deserves our utmost respect and effort to pre-serve. Every species has much to share, a fact that God desires for us to comprehend and appreciate, and much is lost both physically and spiritually when entire species are destroyed carelessly. The classic Christian hymn, "This Is Our Father's World" echoes many of these affirmations, in lyrics like "All nature sings" and "God speaks to me every-where." [4]

> Ever since the creation of the world God's eternal power and divine nature, invisible though they are, have been understood and seen through the things God has made. So people are without excuse; for though they knew God, they did not honor the Creator as God or give thanks, but they became futile in their thinking, and their senseless minds were darkened. Claiming to be wise, they became fools; and they exchanged the glory of the immortal God for images resembling a mortal human being or birds or four-footed animals or reptiles . . . they exchanged the truth about God for a lie and worshipped and served the creature rather than the Creator, who is blessed forever! Amen (Romans 1:20-23, 25).

Here the Apostle Paul confirms even more directly that people can come to know God's divinity and power through the creation—what God has made. A retreat involves helping people consider God, to connect more deeply with God, and to develop faith in God and God's love. The blessing and beauty of the natural world is one avenue that God provides for God's own self-revelation. It can be, in the language of our tradition, a powerful means of grace. Many people sense God's presence when they are in the midst of nature.

However, we must be careful never to worship the natural world itself as if it were God, anymore than we would worship ourselves or another human being in place of God. Some have a misconception that by inviting people to go into natural settings we are drawing them away from God, when the opposite is true. The key to avoiding misunderstanding is to be very clear that nature leads us to recognize and worship the Creator. We never encourage people to idolize animals, plants, the earth, etc., anymore than we would worship ourselves or another human being as God. With this clearly in mind, a part of the opportunities offered by retreats is to lift up the goodness of the natural world and to engage people in spiritual practices that affirm creation as one of the ways through which God loves us, speaks to us, blesses us, and draws us near.

A Source of Wisdom

In addition to "telling the glory of God", scriptures point to the diversity of creatures and ecosystems as sources of Divine wisdom and instruction. Other forms of life can be our mentors and offer essential lessons on life, if we humans are humble enough to be receptive. Here are just a few examples from the Bible of well-known spiritual mentors passing on lessons they gain from time spent observing God's natural world.

> God gave Solomon very great wisdom, discernment, and breadth of understanding as vast as the sand on the seashore, so that Solomon's wisdom surpassed the wisdom of all the people of the east, and all the wisdom of Egypt. He was wiser than anyone else, wiser than Ethan the Ezrahite, and Heman, Calcol, and Darda, children of Mahol; his fame spread throughout all the surrounding nations. He composed three thousand proverbs, and his songs numbered a thousand and five. He would speak of trees, from the cedar that is in the Lebanon to the hyssop that grows in the wall; he would speak of animals, and birds, and reptiles, and fish. People came from all the nations to hear the wisdom of Solomon; they came from all the kings of the earth who had heard of his wisdom (1 Kings 4: 29-33).

When Solomon became king, God asked him what he wanted. Solomon only asked for wisdom to lead the people well. God honored his sensitive request and he became one of the wisest persons who ever lived. A great deal of his wisdom came from lessons gained from observing plants, birds, reptiles, fish, and a plethora of other dimensions of wider community of life. We not only learn scientifically from observing nature. We learn spiritual truths, since it all has its origin in God.

> "But ask the animals, and they will teach you; the birds of the air, and they will tell you; ask the plants of the earth, and they will teach you; and the fish of the sea will declare to you. Who among all these does not know that the hand of the LORD has done this? In God's hand is the life of every living thing and the breath of every human being" (Job 12:7-10).

The author of Job points to nature as a source of insight as he wrestles with his own life experience. As Job dialogues with his friends, he encourages them to turn to the natural world to gain understanding. Part of that understanding is that, "In God's hand is the life of every living thing and the breath of every human being." Another part of the overall message of Job is that, while we may glimpse God in part, we will never fully comprehend all there is to know about life or the Source of Life.

> Jesus put before them another parable: "The kingdom of heaven is like a mustard seed that someone took and sowed in his field; it is the smallest of all the seeds, but when it has grown it is the greatest of shrubs and becomes a tree, so that the birds of the air come and make nests in its branches." He told them another parable: "The kingdom of heaven is like yeast that a woman took and mixed in with three measures of flour until all of it was leavened" (Matthew 13: 31-33).

Jesus himself was a Rabbi familiar with nature, who regularly sought out time in gardens and remote places for prayer, discernment, and renewal. His teaching reflects his observations and their application to spiritual growth and wisdom. "The Parable of the Sower" would be yet another illustration of this pattern.

Creation as Community

> The earth is the LORD'S and all that is in it, the world, and those who live in it; for he has founded it on the seas, and established it on the rivers (Psalm 24:1-2).

For people of faith, this is fundamental. The earth is not ours to treat and do with any way we please for our benefit alone. The earth is the Lord's. We do not truly own our yards, our retreat centers, or our sanctuaries. Our homes are not ours. The wilderness is not ours. We are blessed to have the opportunity to live and to enjoy this community and these places. However, for Christians, private property is a bit of a misnomer. Ultimately, it is all

God's public lands meant for a wide diversity of creatures, as well as human need. We are privileged to be caretakers of what is precious to the one who brings it all into being, and to preserve it on behalf of all creatures for whom God provides, both now and in the future.

It is not always easy to do with less in the balance of giving and receiving so that others may live, but we do so out of love. We are not independent. We are part of something even more profound—interdependence. What is God's desire for the whole earth? That is a question to guide our deliberations, our Christian education, and our actions.

God's Covenants with Creation

"I establish my covenant with you, that never again shall all flesh be cut off by the waters of a flood, and never again shall there be a flood to destroy the earth." God said, "This is the sign of the covenant that I make between me and you and every living creature that is with you, for all future generations: I have set my bow in the clouds, and it shall be a sign of the covenant between me and the earth. When I bring clouds over the earth and the bow is seen in the clouds, I will remember my covenant that is between me and you and every living creature of all flesh; and the waters shall never again become a flood to destroy all flesh. When the bow is in the clouds, I will see it and remember the everlasting covenant between God and every living creature of all flesh that is on the earth" (Genesis 9: 11-16).

The Noah story brings to bear some interesting points. First, if you recall the entire story, it was human behavior that led God to determine that it was vital to make a new start. Just because there was a corruption of what was meant to be does not mean that everything is now worthless. In the story, the message is that God requires the diversity of species be preserved for the future. God actually makes a covenant not only with people; the Lord makes covenant with the earth and every living creature.

The Lord spoke to Moses on Mount Sinai, saying: "Speak to the people of Israel and say to them: When you enter the land that I am giving you, the land shall observe a sabbath for the Lord. Six years you shall sow your field, and six years you shall prune your vineyard, and gather in their yield; but in the seventh year there shall be a sabbath of complete rest for the land, a sabbath for the Lord: you shall not sow your field or prune your vineyard. You shall not reap the aftergrowth of your harvest or gather the grapes of your unpruned vine: it shall be a year of complete rest for the land" (Leviticus 25:1-5).

In this text, we discover the tenet that the land is to participate in periods of sacred renewal and rest. God wants the land, and in extension the natural world, to observe a Sabbath for the Lord. We know that human beings need food and other items for survival, but this does not eliminate the vital call for the natural world to enjoy all that is meant by Sabbath.

> The earth dries up and withers, the world languishes and withers; the heavens languish together with the earth. The earth lies polluted under its inhabitants; for they have transgressed laws, violated the statutes, broken the everlasting covenant. Therefore a curse devours the earth, and its inhabitants suffer for their guilt; therefore the inhabitants of the earth dwindled, and few people are left. The wine dries up, the vine languishes, all the merry-hearted sigh. The mirth of the timbres is stilled, the noise of the jubilant has ceased, the mirth of the lyre is stilled (Isaiah 24:4-8).

When human beings fail to love and to be life givers it not only dishonors God, it affects everything around us. Life is interwoven and interconnected. The creation definitely suffers when human beings are unfaithful. Although this passage is not about industrial pollution, since it was written long before industrialization, its language does have a remarkably modern ring. How much of the earth's current suffering is an outcome of our not living as the children of God? The passage provides an ominous warning about the natural consequences for a people who ignore the ways of love.

A Shared Future

Somewhere along the line, the idea developed that our ultimate future in God has nothing to do with the earth and the rest of creation. This portrait of heaven assumes that only the human soul and its future really matters. Everything else has no lasting value in this philosophy. A complete reading of scriptures, however, does not lead to these conclusions.

> For the creation waits with eager longing for the revealing of the children of God; for the creation was subjected to futility, not of its own will but by the will of the one who subjected it, in hope that the creation itself will be set free from its bondage to decay and will obtain the freedom of the glory of the children of God (Romans 8: 19-21).

The Apostle Paul highlights God's intention for the salvation of the whole creation. As in the beginning we are linked with all of creation, so it shall be in the ultimate future with God. The creation will not simply disappear because it lacks lasting value, as some teach. The creation will be set free, as we will, and with us it has hope in God. Freedom is not annihilation. We are to do our best to manifest now what will fully come in time. The creation is waiting for us to reveal ourselves as children of God in the present, and for us to lead toward that coming freedom for the creation and humanity so eagerly longed for.

> He (The Christ) is the image of the invisible God, the firstborn of all creation; for in him all things in heaven and on earth were created, things visible and invisible, whether thrones or dominions or rulers or powers— all things have been created through him and for him. He himself is before all things, and in him all things hold together. He is the head of the body, the church; he is the beginning, the firstborn from the dead, so that he might come to have first place in everything. For in him all the fullness of God was pleased to dwell, and through him God was pleased to reconcile to himself all things, whether on earth or in heaven, by making peace through the blood of his cross (Colossians 1: 15-20).

In Christ, all things hold together. Through Christ, God is reconciling himself "to all things, whether on earth or in heaven". Unity and wholeness are encompassed in reconciliation. "All things" really does mean all things. Let us remember, also, the famous passage in the third chapter of John (v. 16-17), that declares: "For God so loved the world that he gave his only Son, so that everyone who believes in him may not perish but may have eternal life. Indeed, God did not send the Son into the world to condemn the world, but in order that the world might be saved through him." The term used for "world" is cosmos—the whole cosmos.

Notes

1. *The Works of John Wesley (on CD ROM)*, (Franklin, TN: Providence House Publishers, 1995), Sermon 23—Sermon on the Mount, Discourse 3, Volume 5, page 283.

2. Leonardo Boff, *Cry of the Earth, Cry of the Poor*, (Maryknoll, NY: Orbis Books, 1997), 104.

3. http://www.holdenvillage.org/news/gc2005winter/barnett.html

4. *The United Methodist Hymnal*, (Nashville, TN: The United Methodist Publishing House 1999), hymn 144.

Section Two:
Practices for
Christian Retreats

Introduction

Retreats provide a unique environment for faith formation, renewal, experiences of Christian community, and interconnection with creation. There are a number of retreat elements that contribute to the opportunity for growth in faith, exploration of new possibilities, rest, and enjoyment of the beauty and wonder of God's creation. These encounter practices or activities enhance the retreat experience for participants and enrich the impact of the event on their faith.

It is the purpose of this section to explore a variety of ways for encountering God, encountering others, and encountering creation during the retreat experience. The previous section developed the biblical and theological foundation for retreats. The encounter practices in this section will build upon those insights and observations.

The uniqueness of the retreat environment for Christian growth and formation can be found in several particular characteristics. These qualities offer opportunities for exploring faith that are not usually available in the church building during the regularly scheduled activities. Leaving behind the church building, our regular schedules, the usual way of doing things, and the rush of our daily lives contributes greatly to the meaningfulness of the retreat experience.

Under the best of circumstances, going on a retreat means going someplace else. Certainly that is the recommendation of this book! Retreat participants leave behind the ordinary of their lives and come away to a place apart for the purpose of encountering God, others, and creation. Leaving behind the responsibilities and disruptions of their demanding lives and coming to another place makes possible rest, deeper relationships with others, and the time for reflection on the part of participants. The time and space of retreats spark imagination and creativity. The natural surroundings of retreat facilities are a reminder of the creator God as well as the joy of being God's creatures.

Removed from the hectic pace of modern life, retreat participants enter into a more relaxed environment. Comfortable clothing, conversation around the dinner table, walks in the woods, coffee shared by the fireplace, and time to watch the sun go down all reflect that atmosphere. Such a relaxed environment is an invitation to enter less formal means of study and discussion, worship and leisure. It opens the door for playfulness and laughter. It leads to a consciousness of God's presence in community and creation. It places relationships before tasks to be done. Within the safety of Christian community, people are able to share questions, doubts, and joys more freely and honestly. They may even dare doing things in a new way!

Frequently, church educational and nurture programs put an emphasis on shaping faith through learning information. Schooling techniques and methods using books, papers, and pens are the most common tools for Christian education. The reality that faith is formed and shaped in multiple ways is often overlooked. Instead, the stress is placed on linguistic and auditory learning within a classroom setting. Little recognition is given to the importance of relationships, experiences of Christian community, creation, and spiritual practices.

Retreats, on the other hand, recognize the multiple ways in which faith is formed through encounter practices that nurture the relationship with God, others, and creation. Certainly it is possible to take educational practices that emphasize linguistic and auditory learning into the retreat setting. However, this unique setting also provides the chance to use an assortment of practices that are relational, experiential, and sensitive to the many ways in which people learn to create meaningful and life transforming experiences.

Retreats become natural settings in which to recognize that not everyone learns in the same way. The work of Howard Gardiner has named the ways in which we humans take in information and integrate it. Those who wish to learn more can read Gardiner's book, *Frames of Mind: The Theory of Multiple Intelligences* (New York: Basic Books, 1983).

For Gardner, intelligence isn't limited to the I.Q. of a person. Instead, he understands that intelligence is the ability to create problems to solve and ways to solve them. Each of us has a preferred manner in which to do that best. Gardner has identified at least eight different ways in which people express their ability to create and solve problems:

- Logical/Mathematical
- Intrapersonal
- Musical
- Spatial
- Linguistic
- Interpersonal

- Bodily/Kinesthetic
- Naturalist

Retreat practices strive to be sensitive to these multiple intelligences and make use of all the human senses. Through a variety of activities—movement, music, puzzles, nature exploration, storytelling, journaling—each person can find a comfortable way to engage with the retreat experience.

Within the sustained and intentional community of a retreat, relationships often become more important than mere information about the Bible or church tradition. The emphasis on hospitality, community building, participatory Bible study and worship, storytelling, and enjoyment of nature reflects the high value placed on interaction between participants, God, and the creation. A sense of belonging to the community may be the most significant element of meaning-making for many retreat participants.

Sometimes activities such as recreation, community building games, fun songs, storytelling, and outdoor worship are considered as retreat extras. Even though it is often these activities that draw people to retreats, rather than the more formal study aspects, they are understood as fun activities unique to retreats but not part of the meaning-making elements of faith formation. Rather, during a retreat everything that happens is valued and contributes to the whole! Nothing is less or more important than something else.

The experiences of the retreat participants—both those they bring and those they share—contribute to the uniqueness of retreats. Most of the encounter practices outlined within this section depend on the willingness of retreat participants to open themselves and share their experiences. As people share with each other, they have an experience together. That experience becomes a shared story, a container of the retreat's meaning, insights, laughter, and sense of belonging.

Unlike some educational and nurture activities within the church, everything that is done during a retreat is part of the experience and part of the meaning-making purpose! Every moment from the time participants arrive until the time they get in cars and buses to leave is important. Recreation, community building games, fun songs, storytelling, and outdoor worship are not fringe benefits of a retreat, but the very heart and soul of these experiences. Each element of the retreat experience contributes to a participant's sense of meaning, belonging, and rest from the bedlam of daily life. Each element of the retreat experience has the capacity to enliven encounters with God, encounters with one another, and encounters with creation.

The practices suggested in this section are based on the assumption that every moment carries meaning, and are organized around the three types of encounters discussed in the first section of the book. For each kind of encounter, a bridge is built between the biblical and theological foundation and specific practices or activities that can be included within the retreat experience. Within each encounter section, you will find:

- a rationale for the encounter practice;
- suggestions for specific activities;
- a resource list related to the encounter.

The section concludes with some ideas for bringing the retreat to a close so that participants can move back into their regular lives and integrate the meaning and sense of belonging they have experienced during the retreat.

Encounters
with God

God made us for relationship. God longs for that relationship and has placed within us, as part of our human nature, a yearning to be in relationship with God. St Augustine said that our spirits are restless until they rest in God. God has created us with this capacity and put within us the hunger for union with God. The first step in any journey toward an encounter with God is recognition of that longing. Our desire for God takes us on a search for sacred space, a search for the holy. In the original Hebrew, the word translated as holy means "set apart". As humans, we cannot open ourselves to God without setting aside time from those ordinary, secular parts of our lives and seeking out holy, sacred space and time for God.

There is no question that modern life, as we know it, is chaotic. The pressing requirements of our families and our work surround us; the list of things to be done is endless. The pace we keep, our drive to make ourselves worthwhile, and our constant sense of life as a competition to be won makes our lives crazy. A spirit of frenzy marks even our leisure time!

We long for meaning in our lives and seek answers to the difficult questions of life. "Who am I? How do I fit in? What is ultimately of importance? What is my greatest treasure?" Finding answers to these questions helps us make sense out of our lives and gives us a sense of purpose. Out of these answers, each of us weaves together a fabric that carries our personal sense of meaning. However, in the midst of our busy lives, it is difficult to find the time and space to ponder these important questions.

As a result of our constant movement, we neglect our relationship to God—failing to listen, to sense God's presence, to enjoy God's gifts, to deepen our awareness of God's graciousness. The craziness of each of our lives stands in contrast to the life God intends for us. God's plan for all God's people—and all of creation—is peace, justice, wholeness, and harmony.

It was not by accident that God rested on the seventh day of creation, or that God commanded the Israelites to keep the seventh day separate for rest. In Hebrew, the word Sabbath actually means "to catch one's breathe". In the midst of our lives we need to be intentional about setting aside the time and space for God's holiness to heal and renew us. We need to find ways to step away from the chaos in order to receive the peace and rest God desires for us.

Such an understanding of our need for God and the time and space needed to care for that relationship opens the door for retreat encounters with God that are meaning-making, restful, and relational. However, we must decide to set time aside and seek out the space. The first step of that journey takes place when retreat participants get into their cars or buses to physically leave behind the everyday of their lives and to come away to a retreat setting. The decision to move away is the first necessary step toward encounters with God.

Practices for Encounters with God

Bible Study

In choosing methods for the study of scripture it is important to remember the goal and objectives of the retreat. What is it that you want retreat participants to find at the retreat, and what do you want them to take away with them from the retreat? Only by asking these questions can you choose effective methods for encounters with God through the scripture.

Retreats offer the opportunity to try out a variety of methods for the study of scripture that add an emphasis on experience and relationship, as well as information and content. As you plan for the exploration of scripture, consider the manner in which the following methods invite participants to weave together passages of the Bible with their own experience and to respond by making new commitments to God's good news.

Each of the methods described here creates a dialogue between the experience of the group member and the scripture. They each invite the retreat participant to tell his or her story and to listen to that story within the context of the scriptural story. Within this conversation there is the opportunity to listen anew to God's word and to respond.

These methods go beyond inviting us to learn about God; they open a doorway for God to encounter us through the stories of scripture, observations of God's actions, and engagement of our hearts. Such encounters can transform our faith and our lives.

A Small Group Model for Bible Study

Step 1: Have someone read the biblical passage aloud

Step 2: Each person identifies one word or phrase that catches his or her attention.

Step 3: Each person shares the word or phrase with the group.

Step 4: Have a second person read the biblical passage again.

Step 5: Each person writes down how the biblical passage affects his or her life right now.

Step 6: Each person shares what he or she wrote in #5 with the rest of the group

Step 7: Have a third person read the biblical passage.

Step 8: Each person writes down what God is saying to him or her through the passage.

Step 9: Each person shares what he or she believes God is saying to him or her through the passage.

Step 10: Each person prays aloud for the person on his or her right, repeating what was shared in #9.

Shared Praxis

The Shared Praxis model, developed by Thomas Groome, invites participants to have a conversation between a problem or challenge in their own life and a portion of scripture. Prior to the meeting, select a scripture passage and a topic that the passage addresses. For example, Matthew 4:1-11 describes Jesus' encounter with the devil in the wilderness and addresses the issue of temptation.

Step 1: Encourage group members to share their own experience with the identified topic, for example, temptation. What tempts you? What do you do when tempted? How do you feel? Share a particular time you were tempted and what happened.

Step 2: Invite group members to reflect on what the process of temptation is and what the consequences of their actions are. Why do you think we get tempted? What do you hope to gain by giving in or resisting?

Step 3: Set the biblical story in context and provide any background information important to understanding the story. Read or tell the biblical passage. Invite the group members to discuss what happened in the story. What did Jesus do? What does it show about us and about Jesus? How do you think Jesus felt? Why did he resist?

Step 4: Encourage the group members to have a conversation between the biblical passage and their own experiences. How is Jesus experience like your own? What did Jesus do to help him resist the temptation? How is Jesus a model for us?

Step 5: Encourage group members to think about ways hearing this story and reflecting on their behavior will change their response to temptation in the future. Invite the group members to name specific things they can do in the future to resist temptation.

Creative Responses to Scripture

Step 1: The leader introduces a biblical theme or topic, such as baptism, to the whole group, giving them an overview of the traditional understanding of the topic as well as the interpretation and use the church has made of this topic through the centuries.

Step 2: Divide the whole group into smaller groups of 3-8 people and assign each group biblical passages about the topic to read. Encourage the group to discuss what the passages have to say about the topic. Have the group make a creative response such as a skit, a poem, a prayer, a picture, or a song that reflects their understanding of the topic in light of the scriptures they have read.

Step 3: Gather together the whole group and invite each small group to share their creative responses to the scripture.

Worship

Worship is the central act of the people of God. Early in Genesis we learn that the patriarchs built stone altars for worship. Later, during the reign of Solomon, the Temple in Jerusalem became the center of all worship. The language of psalmists gives us a glimpse of Israel's worship. The command to worship echoed throughout Jesus' ministry and the story of the church. In today's world, we recognize the importance of worship by building sanctuaries set apart for that use alone. For many, Sunday worship is their only contact with the life of the church.

Therefore, no retreat would be complete without times of worship so the gathered community can invite God into their presence with praises, confession, supplication, offering, and the hearing of God's word. Retreats, however, present the community with the opportunity to engage in other forms of worship beyond the familiar Sunday morning format. Morning watch, morning and evening prayers, vespers, and times of silence can be offered as options.

- Morning Watch usually takes place early in the morning, often before breakfast. Retreat participants gather together out-of-doors. A worship leader introduces a focus for the reflection and suggests a psalm, biblical passage, or devotional reading. Participants then move into an outdoor spot for individual reflection on the suggested reading and on a new day with God. A bell or whistle brings everyone back together for sharing of experiences and a closing prayer.

- Morning or Evening Prayers/Vespers are short worship formats. Traditionally, they include the reading of a psalm, a spiritual song, and prayers of intercession. Within the retreat setting they can be used in this way, or as any simple worship to begin and end the day.

- Times of silent worship can be used at any time during a retreat. See more on spiritual practices later in this section.

- A closing worship service (often on Saturday afternoon of a two day or Sunday morning of a three day retreat) provides an opportunity for corporate worship to end the retreat event. Often, this is the time when communion is celebrated. Worship at retreats can use this three-part format:

Gathering includes call to worship, music, confession, thanksgiving, praise.

Hearing the Word includes reading the scripture and reflecting on it.

Responding to the Word includes offering, prayers of supplication, communion, music. It may not be necessary to have bulletins, but post the order so participants will know what will happen next.

Practices

Within the retreat setting, participants can play a part in creating worship elements, such as choosing music, writing prayers, dancing, singing, and serving communion. While it is normative to have the "preacher person" interpret the scripture, encourage participants to join in the reflection on the Word by responding to questions for discussion, or inviting an artistic response such as painting or dancing. The scripture itself can be presented in a skit or choral reading.

The relaxed and informal setting of a retreat suggests an environment for worship that is more relational, participatory, and experiential, as well as less highly structured than Sunday morning within a church sanctuary. Retreat worship enables worshippers to praise God outdoors, to sit in other arrangements, to include movement, and to engage all their senses.

The God who became incarnate in Jesus Christ still encounters us through physical objects and actions. It is only through our senses that we can fully apprehend the movement of God with us. The primary symbols of our faith – water, bread, wine, and the cross – are physical representations of God's person and action. The retreat setting invites participants to explore these symbols "up close and personal" and to encounter their deeper meaning. Here are some ideas of how to do that within worship.

Water

- Place a large bowl of water on the worship center so that everyone can touch the water.
- Place a fountain on the worship center so that people can hear the sound of running water.
- Hold a worship service on the shore of a lake or stream or within view of a body of water so that worshippers can hear, touch, and see the water.

Bread

- Make bread together and use it for communion.
- Have communion immediately following a regular meal around dining tables.
- Use a common loaf for communion.

Wine and the cup

- Invite a local potter to help you make a cup during the retreat.
- Invite children who do not drink from the cup to spread grape jelly on the bread.
- Use one cup and one loaf of bread. Pass it to each other so each person can take a piece of the bread and dip it into the cup.

Cross

- Hold worship at an outdoor cross.
- Read "The Tale of the Three Trees". (Angela Elwell Hunt and Tim Jonke, Cook Communications, 2004).
- Stand or sit in the form of a cross for worship.
- Have each person make a personal cross from nails or wood.

Music

Music plays an important role in the worship of God. Music allows us to lift our voices in praise and joy. The psalmist invites God's people to praise God, "with trumpet . . . with lute and harp . . . with tambourine and dance . . . with strings and pipes . . . with loud clashing cymbals" (Psalm 150). For some, music is the most meaningful way to worship God.

Music within a retreat can include traditional favorites, contemporary praise hymns, fun songs, and new verses set to familiar tunes. Music sets a joyous tone for a retreat, and fills retreats with a sense of praise. When adapted, music expresses the experience of retreat participants and pulls generations together, as the sweet sound of voices rises toward the heavens. Sing during meals and during walks in the woods.

Choose music that matches and enhances your theme and purpose. If you choose music that is unfamiliar to retreat participants, provide song sheets with the words and spend time teaching the songs so that participants feel comfortable singing along. Repeat new songs several times before using them in worship. However, plan a mixture of familiar and newer songs. It is hard for people just to sing new songs and not to include some favorites. It is difficult to sing along when the song is new.

Identify someone who has experience as a song leader. Avoid song leaders who may tend to present a performance rather than inviting and encouraging others to sing along. It is a plus if a musician can accompany singing with a guitar, piano, or harp, especially if the songs are not familiar. Rhythm instruments can also enrich the use of music within a retreat.

Many collections of newer song and praise hymns are available in denominational bookstores. Several are listed at the end of this chapter.

Spiritual Disciplines

Spirituality is concerned with our response to God as a result of the hunger for relationship God created within us. Marjorie Thompson, in her book *Soul Feast*, says "spirituality is simply the *capacity* for a spiritual life . . . the human capacity to receive, reflect and respond to the Spirit of God".[1]

There has been recently a rebirth of interest in the spiritual disciplines and traditions of the church. The goal of spiritual disciplines is to be receptive to the presence of God. While many disciplines have been adapted for our day, their roots are deep within the tradition of the church.

All retreats offer the opportunity for the inclusion and use of spiritual practices. Some retreats focus entirely on the practice of spiritual disciplines. Spiritual disciplines open our way to the presence of God. They provide an avenue for our encounter with God and for nurturing our relationship with God. However, it is important to always bear in mind that we have been called not just to a relationship with God, but also into relationship with others and with all creation. Therefore, spiritual disciplines must never become an individual exercise in personal piety. The purpose of practicing these disciplines is to invite the presence of God with us as we relate to others and to creation. It is probably not an accident that "disciplines" and "disciples" come from the same root word. The purpose of disciplines is to make us better disciples!

The final thing to keep in mind about spiritual disciplines is that they are like any disciplines. We must make the choice to seek God and we must make the effort to learn and practice the disciplines of our choice. While God does still come to us in amazing burning bushes, which transform our lives, it is also true that living in the presence of God requires our constant attention and intention. The journey into scared spaces must begin with putting God's encounter with us at the top of our list.

It is not the purpose of this book to explore the spiritual tradition of the church in great detail. There are many resources available that do that well. However, it is appropriate to take a quick look at several disciplines, particularly as they relate to the ministry of retreats.

Contemplative Prayer

Contemplative prayer focuses on the words that God has for us, rather than the words we say to God. Within the contemplative prayer there are a variety of forms (two are mentioned here), but each of them place the emphasis on listening to God. They recognize the need for silence and for letting go of our own agenda in order to do that listening.

Meditation

This form of prayer makes use of silence and of images. Times of meditation begin with closed eyes, comfortable position, and quiet breathing. During a guided meditation one person serves as the guide for others inviting those who are meditating to see and hear and taste and smell a scriptural scene. In other words, the guide helps them walk into a biblical story and to experience it anew for themselves. Following the time of meditation, participants have the chance to talk about their experience and to share insights.

Lectio Divina

The Lectio Divina is an ancient form of meditation that involves a four-step process for using imagery to look at scripture.

- Step One: Slowly read the scripture. Pay attention to each word and phrase. Be aware of the words and phrases that particularly catch your attention.
- Step Two: Meditate silently on the words or phrases that caught your attention. How do these words or phrases connect with your life and experience? Ponder the words or phrases and be attentive to what comes to your mind.
- Step Three: Respond to that word or phrase with what you are feeling—joy, thanks, praise, remorse, anger, supplication. Write a prayer or poem; draw or paint; dance; journal, etc.
- Step Four: Rest in God's presence. Just be.

Journaling

Journaling provides an opportunity to write down and reflect on our lives and God's activity and presence in them. Some people use journals as a part of their personal spiritual practice; others may appreciate the chance to record thoughts, feelings and insights during a retreat. Opportunities to journal can be a part of Bible study, worship or times of quiet.

Solitude and Silence

The use of solitude and silence has deep roots within Christian tradition. Early in the first few centuries of Christianity, hermitages and monasteries provided the space for those who felt called to lives of prayer to retreat from the world. Within these communities, dedicated to prayer and obedience, men and women practiced living apart with a full-time focus on God. Large portions of the day were spent in silence.

Short-term retreats offer to modern men and women the same option for briefly living apart from the world in order to focus on God, on prayer, and on obedience to God's call. Times for silence and individual prayer can be included in any retreat. Some retreats are intentionally spent entirely in silence so that nothing diverts participants from being attentive to God.

Some retreat centers now include a labyrinth or ancient prayer path. Labyrinths offer a structure for times of silent prayer and meditation.

Resource List

Resources for Worship

All That We Are: An Arts and Worship Workbook by Aimee Buchanan, Bill Buchanan, and Jodi Martin (Bridge Resources, 1999).

Searching for Shalom: Resources for Creative Worship by Ann Weems (Westminster/John Knox, 1991).

Reaching for Rainbows: Resources for Creative Worship by Ann Weems (Westminster/John Knox, 1980).

Thanks Be to God: Prayers and Parables for Public Worship by Glen E. Rainsley (Pilgrim Press, 2005).

Feasting with God: Adventures in Table Spirituality by Holly W. Whitcomb (Pilgrim Press, 1996).

Harvest for the World: A Worship Anthology—Sharing the Work of Creation by Geoffrey Duncan, ed. (United Church Press, 2004).

Touch Holiness by Ruth Duck (Pilgrim Press, 1990).

Bread for the Journey by Ruth Duck (Pilgrim Press, 1981)

Resources for Music

Songs compiled by Yohann Anderson (Songs and Creations, Inc, 1983).

Sing the Faith (Geneva Press, 2003).

New Song (Presbyterian Youth Connection, 1996) Accompanist book, participants book and CD.

New Song, Second Edition (Presbyterian Youth Connection, 1999) Accompanist book, participants book and CD.

The Faith We Sing (Abingdon Press, 2000).

Chalice Praise (Chalice Press, 2003).

Resources for Spirituality

Soul Feast by Marjorie Thompson (Westminster/John Knox, 1995).

Spiritual Formation Workbook: Small Group Resources for Nurturing Christian Growth by James Bryon Smith and Richard J. Foster (HarperSanFrancisco, 1999).

Wilderness Time: A Guide for Spiritual Retreats **by Emilie Griffin (HarperSanFrancisco, 1997).**

Going on Retreat: A Beginner's Guide to the Christian Retreat Experience **by Margaret Silf (Loyola Press, 2002).**

Notes

1. Marjorie J. Thompson, *Soul Feast*, (Louisville Kentucky: Westminster John Knox Press, 1995), 7.

Encounters
with Others

From the opening pages of the Old Testament we hear about the importance God places on relationship. In Genesis 2:18, God says that it is not good that humans are alone. In the gospels, Jesus explained that those who love him are to love their neighbors as themselves. Throughout his ministry, Jesus redefined the meaning of neighbor and demonstrated what loving a neighbor means. In Acts 2:43-47, we find a model of Christian community in the description of the early church's life together.

Within Christian community, people find a sense of acceptance and safety and love, acknowledge diversity, and celebrate common experiences. Within such a community, there is room for differences of opinion and perspective, as well as a desire for the common good. There is an attempt to balance the rights of an individual with the needs of the community. A shared faith in Jesus Christ binds members together.

This understanding of community stands in contrast to what we sometimes experience in our lives, even within the church. This understanding of community offers an alternative to the secular world's values and standards that put an emphasis on competition and achievement as the path to meaning and belonging.

Christian community is born out of the love and acceptance the members offer to each other, made possible by the love and acceptance they have known in Jesus Christ. True community naturally acknowledges and accepts differences. As human beings, we grieve, celebrate, create, wonder, get angry, feel confused, and long for love. These are the common elements of human life and the building blocks of community. The barriers that separate people come falling down when they discover that those who first appeared different are similar to them in many ways.

However, Christian community does not just happen, it must be built intentionally. It is birthed by a willingness to be open to each other and to God. A variety of practices shapes the intention to form community, including hospitality, community-building activities, storytelling, and table fellowship. They promote trust and openness, love, and joy.

Hospitality

Time and time again each of us has the experience of walking into a new group. It may be a committee meeting, a classroom, a party, a church, a support group, or a retreat. Upon entering into a new space and group of people, we ask variations of two basic questions: "Is there a place for me in this group?" and "How safe is it to tell you who I am?" The difference between standing outside the circle of belonging and feeling secure within the circle of belonging is found in the answers to those basic questions.

At a retreat there is an intentional effort made to answer these questions through hospitality and community building. Hospitality addresses the first question through anticipating it and planning a welcoming environment that says, "We are glad you are here". Community building focuses on the second question, enabling retreat participants to move into the circle of belonging within which they have a sense of security and being known.

Hospitality encompasses anything you do that helps people feel welcome, safe, and accepted. It helps folks feel you are glad they have come and that you want them to be comfortable during the retreat. Hospitality is intentional and carefully thought out. It does not just happen.

Hospitality Practices
Before the Retreat

Hospitality begins long before the retreat happens. Through the registration process, you can address the many questions folks have: Where is it? How do I get there? What do I need to bring? When does it start? How long does it last? What will happen? What is expected of me? How much does it cost? An attractive, informative brochure, a list of what to bring, a map to the retreat center, and a clear statement of all the costs contribute to setting a tone of welcome and inclusion for the retreat.

On the Day of the Retreat

Hospitality continues on the day of the retreat. The Retreat Planning Committee should plan to arrive one or two hours before the retreat participants. In this way they can settle into their own rooms, set up an attractive registration area, place signs, catch their breathe, and pray together.

As folks arrive there are a variety of ways to make them feel welcome:

- Have signs telling participants where to park and where to register.
- Have someone available to welcome participants and to answer their questions.
- Provide maps and/or directions to help participants find the meeting room and their sleeping space.
- Offer hot or cold drinks.
- In winter, arrange for a fire.
- Have nametags ready.
- Call people by name as they arrive.

During the Retreat

A sense of belonging requires care and attention to the details of schedule, meals, activities, risk management issues, and expectations of the retreat center. In this way, the task of hospitality continues throughout the retreat experience.

The retreat center staff shares a portion of the responsibility for hospitality. The level of involvement differs from one retreat center to another. Be sure you know exactly what the retreat center you are using will do and what you are expected to do. Designate a person to maintain the communication between retreat participants and the retreat center staff. Know who to talk to or what to do in order to do such things as getting more towels, unplugging a toilet, or emptying the trash. Be sure you know what retreat guests are expected to do at mealtimes and checkout.

Community Building

The purpose of community building activities is to help retreat participants move from outside the circle of belonging to the inside. Community building activities allow members of the group to share who they are in a fun way, and to discover whether they are accepted into the group. Failure to build trust among retreat participants can result in distrust, mere politeness, competition, and apathy. Worries about safety will not be resolved and community will not be born.

The relaxed and informal atmosphere of a retreat lends itself well to play and fun. As people become more familiar with each other through community building activities, they will grow more comfortable sharing with each other about their faith and spiritual lives at a deeper level.

The goal of group building activities is to develop a sense of community by enhancing the comfort level of the group members and deepening their sense of closeness to others. These activities encourage participants to mix and mingle with each other in a safe, non-threatening, and fun way. Group building activities allow participants to share experiences and information with each other and enable people who do not know each other to talk together. They move people from outside to inside the circle of belonging.

Practices for Community Building

Since the goal of community building activities is to deepen a sense of belonging within retreat participants, the type of activities chosen and the order in which they are used is important. Generally, community building activities fall into three categories: gathering activities, mixers, and name games. Many resources for each type of activity are available, and some are listed at the end of this chapter. Become familiar with one or two activities in each category so you can give the directions in your own words without looking at the book. Be sure you have needed supplies ready.

1. Gathering Activities

Gathering activities are the bridge between hospitality and community building. Participants can begin as they arrive and others can join in. Having a gathering activity available as retreat participants arrive for the first session reduces the amount of time people wonder what to do. Gathering activities provide a fun and easy way for people to "test the waters" of the circle of belonging.

Play "Human Bingo"
Prior to the retreat, prepare a bingo-like chart with five blocks across and five blocks down. Within each block write a piece of information that people can find out about each other. This should be easy to share information, such as:

- went to the beach for vacation;
- was born in another state;
- is the oldest child in his or her family;
- has a pet dog.

As people arrive, hand each person a bingo card and pencil. Encourage participants to find people who fall into the category. When the player finds someone, that person signs his or her name on the bingo card. The goal is to fill as many blocks as possible with signatures, as well as to learn about other participants. The game ends when someone fills all the blocks or when the leader calls time.

2. Mixers

Mixers enable retreat participants to mingle with one another and to gather in groups of three to eight so they can learn about each other in a comfortable and fun fashion. Mixers include two parts, the mingling part and the sharing part. "Barnyard Scramble", described below, provides a format for mingling. "Introductions" offers a way for participants to share about themselves.

Play "Barnyard Scramble"

Prior to meeting, choose three or four animals that make a distinctive, familiar noise and write the name of the animals on 3 x 5 cards so everyone has one. Pass out the cards and explain to the group they are to make the noise of their animal and to find all the other people making the same noise. Once all the same animals have found each other, you can have the small groups take turns making their noise.

Play "Introductions"

Put a box of craft sticks or toothpicks in the middle of the table. Ask each member of a small group to take enough craft sticks or toothpicks to make an outline of a house. When everyone has made a house, explain that for each craft stick or toothpick they used in making the house, they will need to tell one thing about themselves. Go around the circle and invite the participants to tell one fact about themselves for each of their craft sticks or toothpicks.

3. Name Games

Many times retreat participants already know each other because of shared experiences within the congregation. In that case, name games are not needed. However, if friends of group members have come, or if the retreat participants do not know each other, the importance of nametags and name games cannot be overstated. For all of us, being called by name contributes to our level of comfort and sense of inclusion within a new group. It contributes towards the answer to the first question of whether there is a place in the group for us. The whole retreat group can play name games if the group is smaller than twenty people. Otherwise, play name games in the small groups formed during mixers.

Make a Name Puzzle

Give each person a piece of construction paper and provide a variety of markers. Have each person write his or her first name down the left-hand side of the paper, lining up the letters one on top of the other. Next to each letter, have the retreat participants write a word or phrase that describes something about themselves, beginning with the same letter. When everyone has completed a name puzzle, invite them to share what they have written. You can attach all the name puzzles together into a "quilt" that represents the whole retreat community and hang it on the wall in the meeting space.

Storytelling

Stories tell us who we are and give us identity. Stories are the way we answer the request, "Tell me who you are." We tell stories about ourselves everyday when we answer the question, "What did you do today?" Whenever we tell someone about an incident, offer our opinion, or describe our experience, we are telling stories. The content of the stories and the priority of one story over another indicate who we are and what we value.

We are always in relationship with others and a part of a particular group of people, whether that group is a family, a race, faith tradition, or a retreat. Our individual sense of who we are is forged within the communities to which we belong. Stories of those communities contribute to our sense of identity as individuals. Like glue, stories—as memories of a shared experience—hold a community together.

The stories of each of these communities aid us in our questions of identity and meaning. As God's people, it is our relationship with members of the faith community who love us and share God's story that enables us to find meaning and a sense of belonging within the Christian faith. Here we find a story in which we can belong and a God in whom we can believe. Before any of us believed, we had to hear the story told in a form and within a relationship that connected with our need for meaning and belonging.

Practices for Story Telling

The retreat environment provides the opportunity for three kinds of storytelling: God's story, table fellowship, and formal exercises in writing our stories.

Telling God's Story

Through a study of scripture and worship, retreat participants can hear the story of God's actions and revelations in the Old and New Testaments. Telling God's story is essential to our faith formation, and in a time of increasing biblical illiteracy, retreat experiences enable the telling of the story in creative ways that will inform participants in a new way. Perhaps they will hear this story for the first time or in a new way!

As retreat participants sit around tables and campfire, there is a chance to remember that long before scripture was written down, it was told as stories. The unique setting of a retreat offers the chance to simply tell the biblical stories as story. The Hebrews believed that whenever a story was told, it happened all over again. Try out different ways of telling—not reading—the stories. Have someone tell the story of a biblical character in the first person. Tell the story and have the listeners fill in the blanks. Use sounds and movement to tell familiar stories.

Table Fellowship

Retreats provide an atmosphere conducive for informal storytelling. One of the principal settings for this kind of personal storytelling can occur during mealtimes as participants sit around tables. We know that Jesus engaged in table fellowship on many occasions, often eating with the most unlikely of people. One of the first acts of the early church was to eat together. The told stories of their own experiences with the Christ around the table; they remembered the last meal Jesus had eaten with his followers around the table.

In our busy lives there is so little opportunity to eat together. Once upon a time, families ate together everyday. Now it is a rare occasion for many families. However, within the retreat setting there is the time and space to just talk, to ask questions, and to tell stories. During an intergenerational retreat, members of different ages can hear each other's stories and make connections across the generations.

Recording Our Stories

In addition to the storytelling that happens informally and spontaneously, more formal opportunities for personal storytelling occur when retreat participants tell or record their personal stories. Write stories or share them through media in the form of video or audio recording. Illustrate stories with photos. Both the telling of the story and the permanent version of it provide a record for families and a tool for personal reflection and faith formation.

Telling Stories Written by Others

There are many books and resources containing stories that transmit important insights in entertaining ways. Storytellers, also, use the stories of others to draw persons into enjoyment and reflection. The best choices of stories are those that reinforce the themes, goals and objectives of the retreat. Stories should always be in good taste and be sensitive to the feelings of others. Again, find ways to tell the stories with sounds and actions so they come alive.

Recreation and Play

The word "recreation" often conjures up images of kickball or tag, played in a schoolyard. Our minds limit the concept of play to children and their games. More and more our idea of recreation has become one of observation. We spend our leisure time on the couch watching others play sports. The emphasis on sporting has been placed on competition and on winning. Even when we ourselves play, the stress is still on winners and losers.

Retreats offer the opportunity to rediscover the wonders of playing just for fun, enjoying the outdoors, and finding joy in activity together. Within this environment the emphasis can be on rediscovery of "re-creation" and a new perception of play for the renewal of our souls. Engagement of our bodies, minds, and spirits makes recreation and play essentials component of retreats. Recreation and play remind us that Jesus told us that we must be as little children when we come into the kingdom!

Non-competitive games and adventure courses explore a wider understanding of recreation within the retreat environment. Both these forms of recreation boost individual engagement and group bonding. They open the door for fun, creative expression, and lots of laughter.

In planning recreation for a group mixed in age and abilities, choose activities that will respect the different abilities represented, as well as the physical limitations imposed by medical conditions. It is possible to plan recreation that matches abilities by choosing games of various activity levels. For example, older adults may enjoy games that involve standing or sitting in place while moving arms, hands, and heads, such as Bippity Bop Bop. On the other hand, youth are going to want to play games with lots of running, such as Elbow Tag. In a mixed group, gear the activity level down for the abilities of the older members or those with different abilities, and involve everyone in limited movement games. Everyone can still have great fun!

Practices for Recreation and Play

1. Non-competitive Games

Unlike traditional games when there is a winner and losers, non-competitive games place the emphasis on having fun, rather than on winning. Games of this kind come in different levels of activity – low, moderate and high. Here are some examples; many more ideas can be found in the resources at the end of the chapter.

Bippity Bop Bop (low activity)

A group of ten to eighteen people stand in a circle with one person in the center. The center person points to somebody in the circle and says, "Bippity Bop Bop." Immediately that person must respond with "Bop" before the center person completes saying, "Bippity Bop Bop." If the person in the circle says, "Bop" first, then that person remains in the outer circle and the person in the center moves and points to somebody else. However, if "Bop," is not said before the center person finishes, then the person in the circle moves to the center.

Variations:

"Elephant 1, 2, 3" involves three people. The person in the center says "Elephant 1, 2, 3," and the person in the outer circle makes the trunk of the elephant (hands clasped in front of nose) while the people on either side use their hands and arms to make the elephant's ears. The last to make their part of the elephant goes to the center of the circle.

"Mac and Cheese" also involves three people. The center person says, "Mac and Cheese" to someone in the circle. That person pantomimes eating macaroni and cheese while the two people on either side of him or her become noodles and wiggle as if they are being cooked. The last person to wiggle goes in the center of the circle.

Knots (low activity)

Eight to twelve people stand shoulder to shoulder in a circle. Each person grabs the hands of two different people across the circle (not the people on either side). Then the group untangles the "knot" without dropping hands. Instead of holding hands, circle members can connect with scarves. By working together the group will unwind to a circle or two interlocking circles. It always works—well, almost always!

Dragon Tail (moderate activity)

Divide the whole group into smaller groups of six to eight people. These people then stand in a line with the hands on the shoulder of the person in front of him or her, making a "dragon". The last person in the line tucks a bandana into his or her back pocket or belt loop. The head of the dragon then dries to grab the bandana from the back end of the dragon while the rest of the dragon tries to keep the head from getting it. When the person playing the head of the dragon grabs bandana, he or she goes to the end of the line.

Elbow Tag (high activity)

Group members form pairs linked by their elbows with the outside arm bent at the elbow. One person is designated as "It" and another person as the runner. "It' tries to tag the runner. However, in this game the runner can become safe by hooking up with the elbow of one of the pairs. The other person of the pair must then let go and becomes the runner. If the runner is tagged then she becomes "It" and "It" becomes the runner.

2. Adventure Programming

Adventure programming includes a wide variety of activities that can contribute to community building. The common thread throughout adventure programming is the opportunity to work together and to learn from the experience. Such adventure experiences can include initiative games, low, and high rope courses. The inclusion of adventure programming can enrich community building and the fun of a retreat experience.

Many camps and retreat centers offer adventure courses. However, it is important to note that leading adventure programming, especially low and high ropes, requires special training. No retreat group should ever attempt to lead a ropes course without a trained facilitator and without following safety guidelines developed by the site. Choosing a facilitator who is trained to lead this type of adventure programming enriches participation in low risk Initiative games.

Fun, cooperation, and trust building characterize initiative Games. They usually involve a group of people in an activity in which the group works together to solve a problem and depend on each other to reach a goal. Success depends on communication with each other. Conversation following the event can help participants understand what happened and what has been learned about how groups work together. The physical risk is low and, if there are props used, they are moveable so the games can be played anywhere.

Initiative games frequently precede low ropes courses. Some experts in the field do not even distinguish between the two. Low ropes generally use obstacles that have been built on an established course. The physical risk for low ropes is often slightly higher than for Initiatives. The goal of both initiatives and low ropes put the emphasis on allowing a group to work together to solve a problem, and then to reflect on what happened in an effort to learn from the experience.

High ropes courses, as may be guessed from the name, involve elements that are built high off the ground. There is more perceived physical risk on such courses, although they may be safer than Initiatives or low ropes. All high ropes courses should rigorously practice safety standards. While initiatives and low ropes emphasize group activities, high ropes experiences stress individual achievement. However, they can become a group experience of a sort when group members encourage and belay each other and then process the experience together as a group.

Resource List

Best New Games: 77 Games and Trust Activities For All Ages by **Dale N. Lefevre** (**Human Kinetics Publications, 2001**).

Community Building Ideas for Ministry with Young Teens by **Marilyn Kielbasa** (**St. Mary's Press, 2000**).

Camps, Retreats, Missions and Service Ideas by Youth Specialties (**Zondervan, 1997**).

Crowd Breakers and Mixers, Vol. I by **Youth Specialties** (**Zondervan, 1997**).

Crowd Breakers and Mixers, Vol. II by **Youth Specialties** (**Zondervan, 2004**).

Everybody Wins: Cooperative Games and Activities by **Samblhava Luvmour and Josette Luvmour** (**New Society Press, 1990**).

Guide for Recreational Leaders by **Glenn Bannerman and Bob Fakkema** (**John Knox Press, 1975, 1998**).

Group Builders: 50 High Impact Ideas to Revolutionize Your Adult Ministry (**Group, 2000**).

Growing a Group by **Lynn Turnage** (**Bridge Resources, 1998**).

Inspire! Ice Breakers and Openers by **Walt Marcum** (**Abingdon Press, 2004**).

Making Fun Out of Nothing at All by **Anthony and Mike Burcher** (**Abingdon Press, 2004**).

More New Games by **the New Games Foundation** (**Dolphin Books, 1981**).

New Games by the New Games Foundation (**Dolphin Books, 1976**).

On the Edge: Games for Youth Ministry by **Karl Rhonke** (**Group, 1998**).

The Bottomless Bag by **Karl Rhonke** (**Kendal/Hunt, 1991**).

Encounters
with Creation

The choice of a retreat location within a natural setting enriches the entire experience. Such a setting, close to the beauty and wonder of God's creation, reminds us of God the creator, inspires awe and thanksgiving, and reminds us that we are called to be caretakers of God's creation. Activities that increase the enjoyment of the natural surroundings and allow for the exploration of the natural world compliment all our encounters with God.

Being in a setting surrounded by natural beauty allows us to ponder what we know about the God of creation. We can be amazed and filled with wonder by the breathtaking splendor and stunning complexity of what God has made and continually sustains. The Old and New Testament witness recognizes that the God who creates is also the God of redemption. We can know the immanent presence of God through what God has created.

Natural settings enable us to remember that we are creatures, made in the image of God; we did not make ourselves. Surrounded by God's creation, we are called to reconsider our relationship to God and the responsibilities of being God's creature. As we live within the community of God's people, embraced by the natural beauty of creation, we are called to reconsider our relationship to the earth and all it's creatures. As one aspect of God's creation we are interrelated and interdependent with all the other parts.

When the extravagant beauty and might of God's creation touches us, whether it is the pristine waters of a mountain lake or the high mesas of New Mexico or the green of the Virginia forests or the abundance of a field of wild flowers, it fills us with awe. Perhaps it is the beauty of the place or the appeal to our senses that the sights, sounds, and smells of the outdoors provide. Perhaps it is the stillness. Perhaps it is our ability to see the power and creativity of God first hand. Surrounded by creation, we open to God in a way we can never be with our rational, logical, objective minds alone.

Being surrounded by creation moves us to give thanks. Whenever we stand on the shores of God's good and gracious creation, thanksgiving becomes our highest and best prayer. Declarations of God's greatness shown to us in creation, and reminders to give thanks, fill the Psalms. Surely we can sing with the psalmist, "O give thanks to the Lord, for God is good" (Psalm 106:1).

Being outdoors, close to the smells, sounds, and sights of nature we can remember that God calls us to protect creation and to use our voices to speak out again misuse and abuse. Human choices continually threaten the future prosperity and sustainability of creation. In order to support our lifestyle choices and consumer habits, humans are polluting the earth's supply of clear water, gobbling up fossil fuels, destroying rain forests, farmland and topsoil, and contributing to the ozone level. Perhaps as creation surrounds us, we will confess our part in the misuse and abuse of God's good earth. Coming away to a natural setting reminds us of God's call to care for and protect all creation.

Retreat Practices for Encounters with Creation

The encounter with creation requires a willingness to literally open the door and move out-of-doors! While it is possible to enjoy creation from the inside through the windows of a building, being outdoors enhances the encounter. The full impact of the environment touches us through all of our senses—the taste of berries, the sight of the hawk against a blue sky, the sound of water gurgling among the rocks, and the feel of the cool breeze blow across our faces.

An encounter with creation does not need to be complicated, nor does it require advanced knowledge of the natural world. The encounter can be as simple as a walk through the forest, or sitting beside the shore of the lake. On the other hand, a retreat experience offers a wonderful opportunity to learn more about interconnections within ecosystems and to observe the delicate details of the created order. Such a setting allows time for considering lifestyle choices that may have an impact on the future wholeness of all creation.

Enjoyment

Here are some simple activities that enrich the enjoyment of the nature world and lead to a sense of awe and wonder in God's amazing works.

- Take a walk. Find an established path at the retreat center that is accessible and appropriate to the needs of the group. Encourage the group members to walk with their eyes and ears open to their surrounds.

- In the winter, observe the patterns in the snow or the effects of freezing temperatures on plants, ground, and water. Look for animal tracks.
- In the spring, look for signs of new growth and listen for the return of migrating birds.
- In the summer, look for wildflowers and use a regional guide to identify them. Always leave four flowers behind for each one you pick.
- In the fall, listen for the crinkle of leaves as you walk and enjoy the bright colors. Collect a variety of leaves to bring back inside. You can preserve them by ironing them between two sheets of waxed paper.
- Star-gaze. Find a way to sit or lay out under the stars. Since retreat centers are often located away from city lights, the night sky is more discernable. Find familiar constellations. Watch for shooting stars. Ponder the vast size of the universe. Give thanks to God.
- Sit beside water. Find a comfortable place beside a body of water. Watch the water. See the colors, movements and reflections. Listen for the sounds of moving water. Look for the creatures that live near the water. Ponder the wonder of water. Remember stories of water in scripture. Think about what the lack of clean water means to humankind.

Stewardship and Care of Creation

Here are some ways to participate in the care of creation at the site and to consider creation-friendly practice that can be followed at home.

- Do a work project at the retreat center. Contact the center director before you arrive and ask about projects your group can do at the center, such as maintaining trails, marking a nature trail, building birdfeeders, etc.
- Find out about what the retreat center does to care for creation. Invite a member of the camp or retreat center staff to talk about way the facility practices good stewardship of creation. Visit the garden, compost pile, and recycling center if included at the site. Work in the garden and participate in recycling.
- Use natural elements for crafts (Of course, avoid disrupting or taking living creatures and plants or causing harm. Be especially careful of species and areas that are fragile). Plan to use natural elements such as leaves, shells, and pinecones in the crafts you include during the retreat.
- Practice good stewardship by using recycled paper for all handouts.
- Pick up all trash before leaving to go home; recycle paper handouts left behind.
- Form a committee to create ways to interpret stewardship at your home church.

Exploration

The more we know about the natural world, the more apt we are to want to preserve and care for it. The retreat experience provides a setting to explore the wonders of creation and the interrelationship that exist.

- Explore an Ecosystem. Invite participants to use all their senses, to explore one ecosystem such as a pond or forest. Walk into the water; stand among the trees. What do you smell? What sounds do you hear? What do you see? What are the colors and textures of the ecosystem? What evidence do you see of the creatures that live there? Share your observations with each other. Invite an expert to help you interpret the data.

- Take a micro hike. Have each group member measure off and mark a twelve-inch by twelve-inch square. Encourage them to study the surface of the ground, and then dig down to discover what exists at different levels. Share your observations with each other.
- Take a sound hike. Stand in one place, and on a piece of paper make a map of the sounds you hear.
- Go bird watching. Use a regional guide to help you identify birds you find on the site.
- Observe and reflect on God's creation. Take a walk to a quiet place in creation. Have participants find a place to sit, and invite them to choose an element of nature to observe closely. After a short time invite, participants to share the element of nature they observed. Encourage them to tell what this aspect of nature tells them about God.

Observing and Listening

God also provides us with insight and wisdom through the natural world. Allow people to observe and listen for a word from God through an encounter with creation.

A Word of God

Take the participants to a quiet natural setting. They will need a pad of paper and pens or pencils. Warn them about poison ivy and other cautions, if applicable to that particular setting. Give them the following instructions in writing and verbally. Answer any questions they may have before they get started.

1. Find a place in the natural world close by where you can see me or easily hear me call, but where you have a space away from others. You will be there for over thirty minutes.
2. Get comfortable so you can be very still and blend in with your surroundings. Remaining as silent as possible, start to scan the natural world around you. Begin far away noticing everything then look closer and closer in, until you are investigating right next to yourself.
3. Choose one plant, animal, insect, rock, or other item from nature in that place to get to know in great detail. Using your pad and paper write down every characteristic that you can see. Look very closely (you may even want to hand out magnifying glasses). Touch it carefully if possible. Write down how it feels. Taste and smell it too, if feasible. Write down every detail you observe. Does it make sounds that you can hear? Describe those sounds in writing. How does it make you feel inside-what emotions do you feel? How is your creature or object connected with or impacted by its surroundings? What does it contribute to other creatures?
4. Give your creature a name that expresses some characteristic or feeling you noticed.
5. Meister Eckhart, a person of faith who particularly loved God's world, once said, "Every

creature is a word from God and a word about God." What does this creature or object from the community of God's creations say to you about life? What might God be trying to say to us through this creature or object? In a little different twist, what does it say about who God is and what God might be like, since God created it? Jot down all your responses to these questions. Quietly return to the group leader when you finish or sit and enjoy, until you see everyone returning.

6. When the participants return, have them share in pairs a bit about their creature or object and what they named it. Ask them to tell the other person what they think God might be trying to say to us about life through the creature or object they discovered. Finally, ask them to share what it might say about who God is, since God created it. Gather the whole group in a closing prayer circle, in which people share what they are thankful for related to nature and God. (Excerpt from *Twists of Faith: Ministry With Youth at the Turning Points of Their Lives*, by Marcey Balcomb and Kevin Witt, Copyright © 1999 Discipleship Resources.)

Each of these activities offers the opportunity to reflect on God's goodness. Stop along the trail and give a prayer of thanksgiving for the beauty and intricacies of nature. Ask each person to tell something they are thankful for. Read selections from Psalm 104 that describe different parts of creation as you walk around. Gather items from nature such as a pinecone, a colored leaf, or a snakeskin and place them on the worship center as a reminder of the amazing nature of the creator God. Sing a song such as "Awesome God" as you stand under tall trees or by a rushing river.

Resource List

Caring for God's Earth, a curriculum resource for adults (Cokesbury 2002).

Creek Stompin' & Getting Into Nature: Environmental Activities by Connie Coutellier and Mary Low (American Camp Association 2003).

Ecology Crafts for Kids by Bobbi Needham (Sterling 1999).

Nature Crafts by Imogene Forte (Incentive Publishers 2004).

Nature-Oriented Activities: A Leader's Guide by Brookhiser, Judy K., Oswald H. Goering, and Betty vander Smissen (American Camp Association, 2005).

Take a New Bearing: Skills and Sensitive Strategies for Sharing Spiders, Stars, Shelters, Safety and Solitude by Phyllis M. Ford (American Camping Association, 1991).

Keepers of the Earth by Michael J. Caduto and Joseph Bruchac (Fulcrum, Inc., 1988, 1989).

50 Simple Things Kids Can Do to Save the Earth by the EarthWorks Group (Andrews and McMeel, 1993).

Section Three:
How to Plan
a Retreat

Developing a Retreat Team

A retreat begins when a congregation starts to think about the role that retreats can play in its whole nurture and education ministry. Retreats begin by exploring the contributions these unique experiences can make in the overall faith formation and spiritual maturity of members. Rather than having retreats just because they seem like a good idea or for something different to do, churches can include retreats as specific ways to deepen the faith of believers and strengthen their understanding of God's call.

The committee charged with the ministry of nurture and education can begin by determining the overall aim of that ministry. What is the goal of nurturing and educating members? What is the role of nurture and education within the total ministry of the church? What will members be able to know and do as a result of nurture and education? What are the program components of that ministry?

By examining the purpose and characteristics of the nurture and educational ministry, congregational leaders can identify the role that retreats can play in reaching their goals. The theological and biblical foundations for retreats found in the section one of the book can guide their consideration of the need for retreats in today's world. Through the consideration of these foundations, a congregational committee can more easily discover their own reasons for offering retreats within the church's ministry. Deciding to include retreats and identifying their overall purpose will contribute to the church's effectiveness in the faith formation of its members.

The goal of this first step is to create a Purpose Statement for including retreats in the overall ministry of the congregation. In order to do this, the education and nurture committee of the congregation (or a work group designated by them) can use the worksheet,

"Why Have a Retreat?" Pondering the questions on the worksheet will enable committee members to think about their own experiences and understanding of retreats.

After each member of the committee has an opportunity to complete the worksheet, they can then share their responses. Based on the individual reasons to hold a retreat, the group can write a Purpose Statement, recording it on a large piece of newsprint. Once the group is in agreement about the statement, share it with other groups in the church and hand it on to any governing bodies in the congregation that needs to act on it to make it policy.

The Next Step

Once a Purpose Statement is in place, a congregation or a group within the congregation is ready to plan the retreat itself. The first step is to convene a committee or taskforce to do that planning. The Retreat Planning Committee is best composed of representatives of the group who will sponsor the retreat. For instance, representative from the whole congregation plan a church intergenerational retreat; youth and youth leaders plan a youth retreat; representatives of women in the church plan a retreat for women. In gathering this committee together, invite people with a variety of skills, such as organization and the ability to pay attention to details, program planning experience, as well as worship, music and recreation leadership. Include several people who have been on retreats before. They can add valuable insights to the work of the committee.

Provide prospective committee members with an outline of the task of the Retreat Planning Committee. A concise job description, including details of responsibilities of committee members and the amount of time that will be required, will let people know what to expect. The amount of time and responsibility involved will not surprise them later. It takes a tremendous amount of time to plan a successful retreat. Don't try to fool potential committee members about the scope of the task in order to get committee members!

A Job Description for the Retreat Planning Committee would include:

- attending the Retreat Planning Committee meetings;
- attending the retreat;
- participating actively in the planning process;
- accepting a specific area of responsibility to be determined by the committee.

The Scope of the Retreat Planning Committee's work would include:

- planning the retreat (date, place, theme, schedule, leadership);
- promoting the retreat;
- registering participants;

- offering hospitality;
- developing program elements and coordination;
- recruiting leadership;
- coordinating worship;
- creating an evaluation;
- establishing and working within a budget.

First Meeting

Agenda

Opening Prayer
Introduction of Retreat Planning Committee members
Community Building
Devotional
A look at the congregational Purpose Statement for retreats
Choice of date for retreat
Selection of retreat location
Review of "Church Retreat Planning Schedule"
Formation of workgroups
Assignment of tasks and target dates
Selection of date, setting a theme, setting a schedule, choosing leadership, etc.
Closing prayer

The first meeting of the Retreat Planning Committee can be held anywhere from a year to six months before the retreat. However, the earlier you begin your planning, the more apt you will be to enlist the leaders you want and reserve the date at the retreat center of your choice.

At the first meeting, invite the committee members to introduce themselves and play one or two group building games found in section two of this book. Encourage members of the group to tell about their previous retreat experiences and to share their expectations for this retreat.

For a devotional you can use one of the scripture passages cited in section one of this book. Ask for God's blessing and guidance on the work of the committee.

During the first meeting of the Retreat Planning Committee, several decisions need to be made. The first one is setting the date for the retreat. This date may have already been established before the committee meets. If not, determine the date immediately. Check the church calendar for conflicts with the congregation's other activities. Be sure the group knows who will reserve the date on the church's calendar.

Second, you need to determine the location of the retreat. Available spaces at camp and retreat centers fill quickly and early (sometimes up to a year in advance) so reserve your space as soon as possible. At this meeting, determine who will be responsible for making that reservation. That person needs to find out if the date is available at the camp or retreat center of your choice and what is required to reserve that date. (See the section on "Choosing a Location" for more information.) Usually a deposit will be required to hold the date. Review the budget and availability of funds. (See the section on "Planning a Budget" for further information.)

Review the worksheet, "Church Retreat Planning Schedule" with the committee. Encourage committee members to indicate their interests and skills for the particular aspects of the planning process. Form workgroups based on these interests and skills of committee members. See handout, "Assignments for Workgroups" for suggestions of the formation and assignments for four subcommittees, including Program, Worship and Music, Promotion and Registration, and Hospitality. Re-assign the workgroup responsibilities as needed so that they match the skills of the group members and are appropriate for your setting. Reach an agreement about which work group will assume the responsibility for each task on the "Church Retreat Planning Schedule" and set a target date for each task.

The next major undertaking by the Retreat Planning Committee is the choice of the program elements of the retreat including theme, scripture, format, schedule, leadership, etc. Have everyone decide on a date for this meeting and get it on everyone's calendar. Encourage members of the Retreat Planning Committee to prepare for this next meeting by thinking about potential themes, formats, and leadership.

If everyone has a copy of this book, ask them to read the sections: "Designing the Retreat", "Encounters with God", "Encounters with Others", and "Encounters with Creation" prior to that planning meeting.

Worksheet: Why Have a Retreat?

What retreat experiences have you had?

How have those experiences affected your faith formation?

What has made those experiences important to you?

In what way might retreat experiences differ from or be similar to experiences within the activities of the local congregation?

Why do you think retreat experiences are important for today's Christians?

Write a Purpose Statement for use within your congregation.

Worksheet: Church Retreat Planning Schedule

Up to One Year Before

____ Select Retreat Planning Committee and choose convener ("Introduction to Your Retreat")

____ Set date for the retreat ("Introduction to Your Retreat")

____ Get the date on the church's calendar ("Introduction to Your Retreat")

____ Reserve a location for the retreat ("Choosing a Location")

____ Establish a budget including cost of space, leadership, supplies, etc. ("Planning a Budget")

____ Make a deposit to reserve the retreat facility ("Choosing a Location")

Six Months

____ Choose a theme and write goals and objectives ("Designing Your Retreat")

____ Design a retreat (Retreat Practices: ("Encounters with God"; "Encounters with Others"; "Encounters with Creation")

____ Set schedule ("Designing Your Retreat")

____ Invite speakers/workshop leaders ("Encounters with God"; "Encounters with Others"; "Encounters with Creation")

____ Develop Policies ("Keeping Participants Safe")

____ Plan promotion of the retreat ("Promoting the Retreat")

____ Make announcements about dates/theme/place ("Promoting the Retreat")

Three Months

____ Develop a process for registration and choose a registrar ("Promoting the Retreat")

_____ Design, print, and distribute a brochure for event ("Promoting the Retreat")

_____ Promote! Promote! Promote! ("Promoting the Retreat")

Two Months

_____ Promote! Promote! Promote! ("Promoting the Retreat")

_____ Stay in contact with retreat facility and send any additional deposits as needed ("Choosing a Location")

_____ Design evaluation forms ("Evaluating the Retreat")

_____ Plan for hospitality details and make assignment list ("Encounters with Others within Community")

One Month

_____ Check with leaders about any special supplies they may need

_____ Check on hospitality details ("Encounters with Others within Community"")

One Week

_____ Check with retreat site about numbers ("Choosing a Location")

_____ Check with leaders about time of arrival and any special needs

_____ Purchase snacks and supplies

After the Retreat

_____ Review evaluations ("Evaluating the Retreat")

_____ Get feedback from committee members ("Evaluating the Retreat")

_____ Prepare written report for next year's committee ("Evaluating the Retreat")

_____ Set time and place for next year

Worksheet: Assignments for Workgroups

Program

- invite leadership
- plan recreation and other special activities
- develop evaluation form
- purchase and collect supplies for program and leadership

Worship and Music

- determine and invite worship leadership
- set the worship space or spaces
- invite musicians
- provide song sheets or books
- plan music
- make arrangements for communion (if desired)

Promotion and Registration

- develop a plan for announcements and registration
- write announcements, create posters, etc.
- design, print and distribute a brochure
- manage budget
- collect registration fees
- make reimbursements

Hospitality

- coordinate with retreat location
- plan welcome at retreat location
- assign sleeping spaces to retreat participants
- plan community building activities and mixers
- give oversight to policies and procedures for risk management
- work with Registration to maintain count for retreat location
- coordinate transportation

Designing Your Retreat

Once the Retreat Planning Committee has met to develop a process for administering the retreat and made assignments for promotion, location, registration, financing, and risk management, it is time to design the retreat itself. That process begins with the choice of a theme.

Choosing a Theme

The choice of a theme is more than a decision about a cute title; it gives a direction and focus to the retreat and affects all parts. The theme identifies the theological concept, biblical idea, or ecclesiastical function that will guide the content of the retreat. A theme, for example, could be "Incarnation" (theological concept), "God's Call" (biblical idea), or "Baptism" (ecclesiastical function).

The best process for choosing a theme is to encourage members of the Retreat Planning Committee to brainstorm ideas. Record the ideas on a piece of newsprint. During brainstorming, add any idea without discussing the merits. After posting all the suggestions, the group may begin the discussion. One idea may emerge as a favorite of the group. If not, invite members of the group to vote for their top three choices. The suggestion with the most votes becomes the theme. Double-check that everyone in the group is energized about this idea. If not, continue the discussion and voting process until everyone is excited about the possibilities a theme offers.

Once a theme has been chosen, encourage the group to brainstorm scripture passages related to the theme. Record these passages as they are suggested. For example, if the group decides on the theme of "Baptism" then the passages identified by the group could include the story of Jesus' baptism from the gospels, selections from Acts about baptism in the early church, and Paul's thoughts in his letter to the churches in Corinth and Galatia. Save this list. This brainstorming will become useful later in the process of creating curriculum and worship for the retreat.

Following the choice of the theme, the group will need to write a Goal Statement for the retreat. This statement describes what the group wants to have happen during the retreat. As the Retreat Planning Committee decides on goals for this retreat, they will want to refer to the Purpose Statement created by congregational leaders giving a rationale for including retreats as an aspect of the nurture and educational ministry of the church. Their goals should be consistent with the overall vision of retreats within the congregation. If the congregation does not have a Purpose Statement, the committee should refer back to their own discussion at the first meeting and the statement of purpose they created.

The Goal Statement for this particular retreat identifies the emphasis and scope of the theme and names the value of the encounters—with God, with others, with creation—possible within the retreat experience. The time a Retreat Planning Committee spends developing a Goal Statement for the retreat will be time well spent. This process allows the Retreat Planning Committee to:

- reach agreement on their hopes for the retreat;
- define what they want to accomplish during the retreat;
- provide direction for the development of all the program elements;
- offer guidance for the leadership;
- suggest categories for evaluation.

On a piece of newsprint, write, "During this retreat, we hope that participants will . . ." Invite committee members to add their hopes for the retreat. Combine any similar statements. While there is no specific number of items this list can include, a list of more than six to eight elements will be difficult to manage and keep track of as the committee continues to develop the design. Once that Goal Statement is complete and the entire committee agrees to it, the group is ready to proceed with the rest of the design process.

Planning Your Schedule

As was noted in section two, everything that happens during the retreat is considered part of the design of the retreat. Everything works together to achieve the goals the Retreat Planning Committee has set. The schedule works to make the retreat meaningful and enjoyable for the participants. When completed, the schedule should reflect the committee's sense of what is important among retreat practices, as well as giving attention to the theme.

Planning the schedule involves putting the encounter practices described in section two together into a design that reaches the goals the Retreat Planning Committee has set for the retreat. Like the many threads in a woven fabric, the encounter practices will be woven together into a whole during the design process, reflecting the Purpose Statement developed for the congregation.

Often, two levels of thinking are at work in the designing a retreat: implicit and explicit goals. Implicit goals relate to the "big picture" purpose of having retreats—the longing for rest, for belonging and for meaning. They are the reasons to go on retreats and are mentioned in the Purpose Statement. On the other hand, there are explicit goals as represented by the theme, the program methods, and leadership of a particular retreat.

Both these levels of goals need to be taken into consideration when designing a retreat. For instance, the explicit purpose suggested by the theme may be to learn about baptism by exploring scripture and asking what it means to be a baptized person in today's world. However, if the implicit purpose is to escaping from the rat race for a weekend, getting to know church members better, and finding some rest, then this purpose will be reflected in how time is spent. The Retreat Planning Committee needs to keep both implicit and explicit goals in mind as they determine the retreat schedule.

The value given to implicit goals and explicit goals will affect the use of time within the schedule in a variety of ways. If the implicit goal of giving participants a chance to rest and get to know others is recognized and valued, then the schedule will allow periods of free time so people can talk informally and have an opportunity for solitude. On the other hand, if the explicit goal of getting youth ready to join the church takes priority, then the schedule will reflect this goal through frequent structured sessions.

If the retreat is understood as just one more way to pass on information about the Bible or discipleship, then the methods for encounters will be similar to those used within the church walls. However, if the planning group wants to take advantage of the informal and relaxed environment of the retreat setting, the encounter practices may by more relational and experiential.

The values of encounters with God, with others within community, and with creation will be echoed in both the schedule and the practices. Schedules that allow time for conversation over meals and walks in the woods display the value of relationships with each other and creation. Intentional inclusion of group building activities and play show the importance of creating community and having fun. The introduction of spiritual disciplines and opportunities for time alone will reflect a value for exploring new ways to experience God.

Make a Schedule

In setting a retreat schedule, there are some givens based on the requirements of the retreat facility for things such as times for meals, check-in, and check-out. These set times should be the beginning point for the schedule. Be sure to find out the following information before beginning your schedule:

- What time can you arrive? What time will the rooms be available?
- When do you have to be out of the facility?
- What times can you have access to special equipment or facilities such as canoes or the gym or swimming pool or a hayride?
- What times are the meals served?
- Are guests expected to set and clear tables? Be sure to include time for them to do that.

Next, you will need to decide when to begin registration and when the retreat will conclude. Once you have set the arrival and ending times, mealtimes and special activities offered by the retreat facility staff, then you are ready to add the encounter program elements. Include:

- How many program sessions—keynotes and small group—will you include?
- What times will they be held? How long will they last?
- When will worship be held?
- When will times for community building, recreation and free time be scheduled? How much time will be included for each?

When the schedule is complete it will look very similar to the examples given in the sidebars. During the next few months, the workgroups of the Retreat Planning Committee will develop the services of worship, plan music, choose group building and recreation activities, and tend to the details of hospitality. They will make the specific plans for each element of the schedule.

Sample Schedules

Three-Day Weekend Retreat

FRIDAY

 7:00 — Registration and Getting Settled
 8:00 — Community Building Activities, Announcements and Introductions
 9:00 — First Keynote Address, Introduction to the theme
10:00 — Worship
10:30 — Snacks
11:00 — In Cabins (or facilities)
12:00 — Lights Out

SATURDAY

 7:30 — Morning Watch
 8:00 — Breakfast
 9:00 — Community- building Activities and Second Keynote
 9:45 — Small Groups
10:30 — Workshop using Creative Arts
12:00 — Lunch
 1:00 — Community Building Activities and Third Keynote
 1:15 — Small Groups
 2:30 — Workshop using Creative Arts
 4:00 — Free Time
 6:00 — Dinner
 7:00 — Sharing of the Workshop Experiences
 8:00 — Community Building Activities and Fourth Keynote
 8:45 — Small Groups
 9:30 — Worship
10:00 — Snacks and Social Time
11:00 — In Cabin
11:30 — Lights Out

SUNDAY

 7:30 — Morning Watch
 8:00 — Breakfast
 9:00 — Small Groups Plan Worship
10:00 — Closing Worship with Final Reflections on Theme
11:00 — Go Home

Two-Day Weekend Retreat

FRIDAY

7:00 – Registration and Getting Settled
8:00 – Community Building Activities, Announcements and Introductions
9:00 – Introduction to the Theme
9:30 – Worship
10:00 – Snacks
10:30 – In Cabins (or facilities)
11:00 – Lights Out

SATURDAY

8:00 – Breakfast
9:00 – Morning Worship
9:45 – Community-building Activities and Small Groups
10:30 – Workshops
12:00 – Lunch
1:00 – Community Building Activities and Small Groups
1: 45 – Workshops
2:30 – Recreation
5:00 – Small Groups Plan Worship
6:00 – Dinner
7:00 – Worship
8:00 – Go Home

Two-Day Weekend Retreat

FRIDAY

6:00 – Registration and Getting Settled
6:30 – Dinner
7:30 – Community Building Activities
8:00 – Introduction to the Theme
8:30 – Worship
9:00 – Snacks and/or Bedtime until Whenever

SATURDAY

7:30 — Morning Devotions (optional)
8:00 — Breakfast
9:00 — Large Group Meeting, Singing and Worship
10:00 — Community Building Activities and Small Groups
11:00 — Workshops in Nature Study or Creative Activities
12:00 — Lunch
1:00 — Free Time/Recreation
2:30 — Small Groups
3:30 — Worship
4:30 — Go Home

Within the schedule are also times designated as program sessions that give intentional focus on the theme. It is during these times that participants will expand their knowledge and understanding of baptism, God's call, church membership, spiritual gifts, or whatever the planning group has chosen as the theme. There are a number of options for composing and leading these sessions.

Models for Leadership

There are three basic models for leadership of program sessions you may consider. The decision concerning a model for leadership needs to reflect both the explicit and implicit goals of the retreat. The model for leadership needs to be consistent with those goals. For example, if the implicit and explicit goals of the retreat relate to building community within a congregational group, then having a keynote speaker on theological doctrine would not be appropriate. Rather, use an experiential and relational model.

Keynote

In the model, one or more people are invited to speak to the group. The emphasis is on content. It assumes that the leader has information to give members of the group and the focus of goals is for the participants to learn this information. A leader for this method is chosen based on his or her knowledge of the topic and ability to speak and engage a group of people. This model puts the emphasis on the spoken word and on a linguistic learning preference.

Part of the expectation for this leader is that he or she will have control over both the content and the presentation of that material. The planning group should provide some input regarding their reason for choosing the theme and their goals, (as well as the list of related scriptures developed earlier by the committee) but after that the development of the theme is in the hands of the keynote speaker for their portion of the experience.

When a keynote speaker does not incorporate relational and experiential encounter practice, then these aspects of the retreat need to be carried out by the planning committee during periods beyond the keynote sessions. Choosing a keynote leader who values and supports the communal and relational aspects of the retreat will create a much better coordination and overall experience.

Experiential or Relational

After receiving directions about what to do within a small group, participants spend the bulk of the time researching, interpreting and responding to the theme. Participants work in small groups and develop ways to report back the results of their time together to the large group. This method places a value on the experience of the participant and on developing relationships within that small group and the whole community of people.

There can be one leader who plans and gives direction for the small groups, or there can be leaders who facilitate the activities in each small group. The leaders for this model can come from within or outside the congregation. An essential skill for these people is an understanding of experiential models and a trust in their value for faith formation. The work of the small group may not be limited to discussion, but can involve creative, interactive, or outdoor activities that recognize the many ways people learn.

The Bible study methods suggested in the encounter practices in "Encounters with God" are examples of experiential and relational Bible studies. They value the input, interpretation, and response of the participants, rather than on the content provided by an expert, keynote speaker.

Plenary and Small Groups

A third model combines the first two. A speaker or designated leader presents information about the theme and the participants work together in small groups to respond to the information. The plenary leader will then provide questions or instructions for the small groups to follow. Sometimes the small groups have leaders who have been trained to lead the discussion. Again, it is possible that the response to the plenary will include active and creative activities.

Determining Curriculum

The word *curriculum* is usually defined within the church as print resources for particular learning settings. The word is most frequently used in reference to resources for the church school time on Sunday morning. However, it is also possible to have curriculum for other settings, such as retreats. In thinking about the models for leadership, a Retreat Planning Committee may decide that rather than invite an outside leaders who would plan the theme sessions of the retreat, they would like to lead the retreat themselves.

Obviously, the easiest thing for the planning group is to enlist the skills of a leader to put the whole thing together. However, there are times when the costs of hiring a leader prohibit that choice. In this case the group has three choices: they can use a purchased retreat curriculum, adapt a church school curriculum, or write their own.

Some curriculum, designed specifically for retreats, is available through denominational bookstores. However, for the most part, these are intended for either youth or spirituality retreats. Some resources give step-by-step plans, with plenary presentations and instructions for small groups. Others just suggest activities and let the users put them together. Several are suggested at the end of this chapter.

A second choice is to adapt a curriculum designed for use in church school. This requires the planning group to pick and choose among activities and appropriate resources for the retreat setting. Another option is the use of material prepared for small group ministry. Both these types of curriculum are developed with a few learners in mind and will need to be rewritten for a large group. Adapting curriculum can be a time consuming process but can be beneficial if you pick and choose what works best in the camp and retreat setting and then add your own ideas and activities to enhance the theme.

The advantage of writing your own retreat curriculum, which is another good option, is that the planning group or its representatives can use some of the encounter activities suggested in this book and in other resources to put together a curriculum that specifically meets the goals for the retreat. Refer to the list of biblical passages developed earlier by the Retreat Planning Committee and incorporate it into the curriculum.

A helpful guide for designing the theme sessions is *Teaching Today's Teachers to Teach by Don Griggs* (Abingdon, 2003). This resource provides a pattern to use within each session and includes information about writing session goals and objectives. Although it is not written specifically for the retreat setting, it does provide valuable guidelines for the novice curriculum writer.

Inviting Leadership

Once the Retreat Planning Committee has identified implicit and explicit goals, chosen a theme, and decided about an appropriate leadership model, they are ready to invite retreat leadership. If the person you want to invite is a popular retreat leader, a busy pastor, educator, or seminary faculty, contact him or her as far in advance of the retreat as possible. Popular and busy leaders fill their speaking engagement schedule fast. Even if the person is not well known, you can count on the fact he or she will be busy and have other commitments to honor. So invite the leader as early as possible—even two or three years ahead is not too early.

An essential characteristic to keep in mind when deciding on a leader is that person's experience leading retreats and understanding of the retreat setting. A pastor accustomed to preaching or a professor used to giving lectures may not be the appropriate choice for retreat leadership. The leadership choice needs to be made based on your goal for the retreat and not how well known or popular someone is.

By inviting a leader early in the process, that person can also participate in the later portions of the retreat design. For example, the focus of worship services can be coordinated with what happens during theme sessions. One way or another, this person needs to be familiar with the goals you have set for the retreat and any expectations you have for him or her.

In making an agreement with a leader, be sure to be clear about payment. The leader needs to know whether room and board at the retreat center is included as well as travel and other expenses. It is a courtesy to provide a private room so he or she can have a personal space for down times and preparation.

Resource List

Salt and Light: Youth Retreat Designs, **Presbyterian Youth Connections, (PC USA) 2001).**

How To Conduct a Spiritual Life Retreat by **Norman Shawchuck, Rueban P. Job and Robert G. Doherty (Upper Room 1986).**

Camps, Retreats, Missions and Service Ideas by **Youth Specialties (Zondervan 1997).**

Retreats from the Edge by **Paul Harvey and The Edge Ministries (Abingdon Press 1998).**

Be Still by **Jane Vennard (Alban 2001).**

See also **www.upperroom.org** for small group study curriculum.

Planning
a Budget

One of the first actions a Retreat Planning Committee will need to take is to create a budget or financial plan. The people responsible for managing the money at the church will want to know how the expenses of the retreat will be paid; the people attending the retreat will want to know how much it will cost. In order to determine those two things, the committee as a whole or a workgroup charged with the responsibility will need to collect information about costs and available funds from the church. Then project the anticipated number participants, including their ages, and estimate income for the budget.

Susan Hay reminds us that financial decisions and priorities "reflect what the church values in it ministry. The finances should support and sustain the vision of the church, not determine the vision."[1] As the committee analyzes costs and expenses for the retreat, they should prioritize the expenses in light of the purpose, goal, and objectives. In making choices about how to spend money and the amount of money to be spent, the value of the retreat experience should guide the committee. How much to spend on accommodations, leadership, and program supplies will be determined by the manner in which they assist the planning committee to reach the purpose, goal, and objectives.

If the retreat will be held in the next calendar year, make a budget request through the appropriate channels. If this is the first time the church or group is doing a retreat, you may want to ask the church to make a financial commitment that will assist in getting it off the ground.

Establishing a Retreat Financial Plan

In creating a budget, you will want to know:

- whether there is money allotted in the church budget for the retreat;
- how much the retreat facility will charge per person for housing and meals;
- how much you will owe the retreat facility if fewer people come than estimated;
- whether you will offer scholarships and how much they will be;
- the costs of room and board for leaders;
- other possible sources of income;
- what program expenses need to be included in the budget (snacks, crafts supplies, fee for ropes course, etc.).

Not knowing ahead of time how many people will attend comprises one of the unique challenges of creating a financial plan for a retreat. Unfortunately, both the facility reservation and the financial plan will have to be based not on hard figures but on an estimate. If retreats have been held in the past, use those average numbers. Otherwise, the committee will have to make a guess based on the verbal interest expressed by congregational members. Periodically adjust the financial plan during the planning process to accommodate the real data about numbers and ages of retreat participants as they register and begin to pay their deposits.

Use the worksheet "Establishing a Retreat Financial Plan" to assist you in the planning process. In the income column, enter any amount that has been designated in the church budget for retreats. Then enter the average from previous retreats (or your guesstimate) and multiply that number by the cost per person for meals and beds from the retreat center. Finally, add any other miscellaneous income sources. These figures together provide an idea of the expected income.

In the expense section of the financial plan, place the same figure for housing and meals multiplied by the average or guesstimate of participants you used in the income section. Then make an estimate of costs for program supplies and leadership.

When you have completed the worksheet you will have an estimate of the total cost. If the income and the expense columns balance, the committee should sing the "Doxology", and continue with its planning. However, if the expense column exceeds the income, further decisions will need to be made. You will need to figure out either how to increase the income or how to reduce the expenses.

A number of options exist to increase income. Each of them depends on the policies and traditions of your local congregation. You can:

- increase the price of the retreat for each person to include the leadership and assorted programs costs. Divide the deficit among all the retreat participants;
- hold fundraisers such as car washes, bake sales, etc.;

- appeal to the governing board of your congregation for additional financial support. Be ready to interpret the value of the retreat for the faith development of the congregational members;
- make a request to other committees of the congregation to contribute excess funds from their budgets. For instance, there may be line items in the Christian education and/or formation budgets that can legitimately be used for retreats;
- solicit donor funds.

At the same time, review the expenses you included in the first draft of your financial plan. Examine each expense regarding the manner in which it supports your purpose, goal and objectives. Prioritize among expenses. For example, the committee may find that spending several hundred dollars on elaborate and expensive purchased snack trays each evening is not important to the overall purpose of the retreat. Instead, participants can be asked to bring snacks.

Reaching the goal of balancing income and expenses depends on everyone working together to analyze and prioritize the expenses and honoring the financial plan once the committee has agreed on it. That means that committee members are expected to manage their money, to ask for an adjustment as needed, and to be faithful in the stewardship of the funds allocated to their area of responsibility.

Notes

1. Susan Hay, "Budgeting for Education and Formation Ministry", *The Ministry of Christian Education and Formation*, (Nashville, TN: Discipleship Resources, 2003), 97.

Worksheet: Establishing a Retreat Financial Plan

Income:

Amount allocated in congregational budget   _____

Number of people (average of past retreats or estimate)   _____

x price per person for housing and meals at retreat center   _____

Other sources of income:

_____   _____

_____   _____

_____   _____

Total Income: _____

Expenses:

Number of people (average of past retreats or guesstimate)   _____

x price per person of housing and meals at retreat center   _____

Other food (snacks and communion elements)   _____

Recreation and craft supplies   _____

Leadership (Honorarium and expenses)   _____

Scholarships   _____

Transportation (if provided)   _____

Promotion and Registration   _____

Curriculum (if purchased)   _____

Committee Expenses (refreshments at meeting, travel to
      visit sites, etc)   _____

Total Expenses: _____

Choosing
a Location

The choice of location and facilities for your retreat is a significant one. The hospitality, meeting room, sleep space, and the food can contribute to the success and meaningfulness of a retreat. On the other hand, lack of hospitality, uncomfortable, inconvenient or dirty meeting and sleeping space, and terrible food can detract from the enjoyment of all those who attend.

The location of your retreat is also an important element in supporting the purpose of your retreat and helping you reach your goals and objectives. If participants do not have their needs for basic comforts met, and do not feel safe or welcomed, they will have a difficult time focusing on the spiritual dimensions of the retreat. If there are constant interruptions from other guests, cell phones, and family demands, those attending the retreat will be less apt to engage in the experience. If equipment is not available, space is limited for small groups, and meals are late, the flow of the retreat will be disrupted. In the case of any of these disruptions, community will not be nurtured and positive stories will not be shared.

Types of Retreat Facilities

Many times congregations choose to go to a camp, conference, or retreat center owned by their governing body because it is easy to get to, they want to support the ministry, or they "always" go to this facility. The familiarity of this site offers a sense of "going home" to those who have been there before that enriches the retreat experience for them.

They know what they can expect and may be acquainted with staff members who welcome them each time they come.

However, some congregations either do not have a familiarity with their governing body's camp, conference, or retreat center or simply do not have access to such a facility. In such a case, retreat leaders need to seek out facilities available in their area. Finding a facility that meets your needs necessitates asking questions, visiting one or two sites, and deciding exactly what amenities best serve your particular retreat purposes.

- The search for a retreat location begins by defining your needs. A look at your purpose, goal, and objectives should give you ideas:
- Do you need private sleeping rooms, a big games field, comfortable chairs in the meeting space, or special diets?
- What are the ages of persons attending your retreat?
- What physical needs do they have?
- How far will retreat participants need to travel?
- Can you provide transportation?
- Will retreat participants spend a long time in their rooms on individual tasks?

Spend a few minutes to write down all the amenities you would like to have. Identify the ones most important to you and the ones you can live without. This will give you an idea of what questions to ask when you contact facilities. Although you may not find one place that meets all your specifications, you will be able to locate a facility that meets many of them. Time spent identifying priorities will pay off in the long run.

Once you know what you need, gather information about the options in your area. The Yellow Pages, either in hard copy or on the web, friends who have gone on retreat, and online directories of camps, conference, and retreat centers are the best way to begin. Choose those that seem to meet your requirements to contact by phone. Have your list of questions ready and explain you are just gathering information. However, do find out if

Websites for Directories of Camps, Conference and Retreat Centers

www.clba.org/campsconf.html
www.epicsopalchurch.org/8020_59303_ENG_HTM.htm
www.pcusa.org/pccca/alpha.htm
www.gbod.org/camping/map.asp
www.elca.org/dcm/camps/search.asp
www.mhsc/encyclopidia/contents/C32ME.html

the date for your retreat is available. There is no sense keeping a location on your list if the date is already filled!

Congregations sometimes choose a hotel or commercial conference facility for their retreats. For adults who wish to have comfortable beds, private bathrooms, and a variety of meal choices, such a facility may provide an ideal choice. Many church-related camps and retreat centers are not able to provide these kinds of creature comforts. As a matter of fact, many older adults may choose not to attend a retreat at a more primitive facility because these comforts and accessibility are not available.

However, while hotels and more public centers do provide a comfortable bed, privacy, and interesting menus, they do not offer many of the qualities often valuable to the retreat experience. Hotels are public places serving many people simultaneously. Retreat participants will need to mingle among other guests, so it is harder to build a sense of community. Hotels come equipped with televisions, phones, and computer hookups. If one aspect of the retreat's purpose is to get away from the distractions of everyday lives, it is more difficult when all the temptations and distractions of modern media present themselves to participants.

In the same way, congregations also choose to hold a retreat in their church basement or educational building. While convenient and inexpensive, staying home does not present participants with the opportunity to leave behind the demands and disruptions of their lives so essential to the retreat experience. Since people can come and go easily, sleep at home, and be interrupted by the requests of family and friends, the significance of community building and being away are eroded. If a one-day retreat is planned and time is limited, consider going to another area church. Ask participants to plan to stay for the whole event and leave their cell phones at home.

First Contact

Most church related camp, conference and retreat centers take seriously the ministry of hospitality. They understand themselves as partners with you in your ministry and want to do everything they can to make your retreat a meaningful experience. This spirit of service and welcome should be evident from the first contact you make with a site. Normally, it is safe to assume that the person on the other end of the phone is committed to helping you make your retreat comfortable, successful, and meaningful. If you do not get this impression immediately, you may want to reconsider the use of this facility.

If you are familiar with the site and are calling to make a reservation, then you are ready to check on the availability of the dates you want and book those dates. If you are calling to gather information, refer to the list of amenities you seek. Use the questions suggested on the worksheet as they apply to your needs.

Get Costs

Obviously, one of the most important questions you have for any retreat facility is the cost. Church funds for retreats are often limited. Since the cost is passed on to individuals and families attending the retreat, churches want to keep costs manageable and affordable. You may have to choose between one location and another based on the cost. Unfortunately, sometimes the money issue has to take priority over the appropriateness of the facilities for the purpose of the retreat.

Rate sheets for church related camps, conference, and retreat centers frequently provide separate costs for meeting space, beds and meals. Sometimes discounts are available for families and children under a certain age. Beds are sometimes counted per individual bed; sometimes you rent a whole building and all the beds whether you use them or not. At some conference and retreat facilities, churches of the denomination owning the site receive one rate system while corporations or other denominations receive a higher rate scale. Since camps and retreat centers offer such a wide variety of options and combinations, these rate sheets can be confusing! Often, camp and conference centers put price packages together to meet the needs of the group. The office staff member who works with reservations can interpret the pricing system and develop a package to meet your needs.

Hotels will reserve a certain number of rooms for you and will expect you to pay for the rooms you reserve, whether you use them or not. Unlike hotels, most church-related facilities make reservations based on an estimate of the number of people who will attend. Since your reservations will be made up to six months to a year before the event, you will not have exact numbers at that point. Church-related facilities usually work with you to adjust numbers up and down as the date of the retreat approaches. However, be sure you know from the beginning the minimum numbers requirements and the consequences if you fail to meet that minimum.

In most cases, the camp or retreat center will ask for a deposit and the completion of a registration form before confirming the dates. Depending on the policies of the center, you may have to pay half of the fee before the retreat and the remainder following your event. Facilities also have cancellation polices that allow you to cancel your event and receive a partial or complete refund of your registration fee. Be sure you understand the policies of the center regarding payment of fees and timeframe for making changes to your numbers. The policy should state this information clearly on your registration form. If not they are not clear, be sure to ask.

- When you make you reservation, be sure to find out what the fee includes:
- Are such things as snacks, flipchart paper, audio-visual equipment, hayrides, campfires, canoeing, etc. included in the basic fee, or will you be charged extra?
- Do you have to build your own campfire, or will a staff member do that?

- If the facility has a high or low ropes course, how much does it cost to use this program area and the services of the instructor?

These fees can add up and affect the final price. It is better to find out ahead of time than be surprised when the bill arrives!

Visiting the Facility

If you are not familiar with the facility for your retreat, it is a good idea to visit it before the retreat. Most church-related camps and retreat centers gladly will show you around the facility. You may want to visit before making a reservation to see the meeting and sleeping options, and ask questions face-to-face with a staff person. Such a walk-around will give you an opportunity to actually see the facilities and determine whether they are appropriate for your needs. You will also be able to get a sense of the "spirit" of the place.

- Do they take hospitality seriously?
- Do they understand what they do as ministry?
- Is the facility clean and well maintained? Is the dining room attractive and conducive to community building?
- Are staff members committed to supporting you in your ministry?

It is also a good idea to visit the retreat center before the time of the retreat, if you have never been there before or been responsible for leadership of a retreat. Walk through the meeting space with a staff member. Find out when you can arrive and begin to set up the room. Ask about other supplies or equipment the facility has. Double check on what the staff provides and what you need to bring. Encourage the staff member to tell you about any other groups that will be sharing the facility with you. Determine which program areas need to be coordinated with that group or groups. Decide how to set up registration and how you will provide hospitality for retreat participants as they arrive. Be sure you know where the sleeping areas are so you can direct church members without having to find a staff member. Get maps of the facility ahead of time so you can mark the buildings you will be using and distribute them to retreat participants as they arrive.

Since church-related camp, conference and retreat centers understand their role in making your retreat meaningful, they will help you as you do your planning. Do not hesitate to call or email to ask questions or to confirm your understanding of their expectations and policies. Retreat center personnel work with a wide variety of groups and can often make suggestions about ways to solve problems, or can lead you toward resources that will enrich the experience. No question is too dumb; every request is taken seriously. If the person in the office is not able to help you, ask to talk with the director who may have access to additional resources.

Worksheet: Choosing a Retreat Location

Name of Retreat Center _____

Phone Number _____

Meeting Space

What size are the rooms? Is electronic equipment provided, such as TV/VCR, sound system, wireless, and projectors? Are the facilities handicap accessible? Who sets up the room? Are guests responsible for cleaning facilities at the end of their stay? Are flipchart and markers available? Included or for a fee?

Sleeping Facilities

How many beds to a room? Are bathrooms in the same building as the beds? Are there private bathrooms for each room? Are linens provided or do guests need to bring their own linens or sleeping bags? Does the facility provide a "What to Bring List"?

Meal Options

Can guests cook their own meals? Are plates, silverware, and cooking utensils provided? How are meals served? Cafeteria or family-style? Is the facility able to provide for special diets? Will your group need to share a dining room with other groups? Are snacks available? Included or extra?

Outdoor Recreation Facilities

What outdoor activities and facilities are available such as campfire circle, canoes, volleyball, high and/or low ropes course, swimming pool, etc? Is there an extra fee for the use of these facilities? Does the site provide a lifeguard or ropes facilitator? Do guests need to bring their own firewood?

Minimums

Is there a minimum number of people required?

Promoting the Retreat

Time is precious to people in our busy, hurried world. Many options and activities are available to them and they must make choices about which ones they will participate in and how they will use their time and money. People engage in activities that offer them meaning, a sense of belonging, and enrichment to their lives. People long to get off the merry-go-rounds of their lives and find a place of rest. People hunger for God and for a deepening of their faith.

In promoting the retreat, prepare to answer the question, "Why should I use my time and resources to attend this retreat?" Begin with the purpose statement and interpret the purpose, theme, and focus so your answers respond to this question. The retreat may not meet the needs or hungers of everyone; that is okay. However, by being clear from the beginning what people can expect, you will reach those seeking what the retreat does offer.

A Plan for Inviting the Congregation

Develop a comprehensive plan for communicating with the congregation about the retreat. This is the first task for the Promotion Workgroup. Before a single notice about dates gets put in a bulletin or newsletter, the group should lay out a timeline for announcements and the registration process. This plan includes tasks, target dates for completion of the task, and the person responsible for completing it. Frequent meetings will enable the workgroup to keep track of its progress.

Charge this workgroup with two basic responsibilities: announcement of the event and registration for the event. Each of these responsibilities has a unique purpose. The first task relates to communication of information about the retreat, what people can expect and why they should plan to participate in the experience. The second enables people to actually sign up to attend the retreat. These two tasks are closely related to one another and need to work seamlessly with each other.

Methods of communication, or tools, exist for each of these tasks. Part of a strong plan for supplying information about the retreat consists of identifying the appropriate tools for each task. Posters, newsletters, bulletins, and announcements during worship tell the congregation about the retreat. Use these tools to convey the date, times, place and theme. However, a registration process including a brochure is necessary for congregational members to actually sign up to attend the retreat.

Tools for Getting the News Out

Many creative and innovative ways exist to get the word out about the event. Take advantage of all the electronic and media resources available for developing publicity and for communicating with church members. Make use of color, photos, and graphics. Use the expertise of people who are familiar with these resources and who work with them on a regular basis.

Choose a look for all communication about the retreat. By designing a "brand"—a consistent graphic look—for the retreat, you tie everything together and church members will be able to easily identify all the communication about the retreat. Select a graphic image or logo that reflects the theme of the retreat or the name of the retreat, such as "Annual Church Family Retreat". Use this image whenever you make announcements in print, on the brochure, on the poster, and on items associated with the retreat such as t-shirts.

As noted earlier, one of the first things the Retreat Planning Committee needs to do is put the date of the retreat on the church's master calendar. Congregational members need to know those dates as soon as possible, so they can get them on personal and family calendars. It is never too early to announce those dates! Although church members do not need to know where the retreat will be held at this point, it is a good idea to confirm the location before announcing dates.

When the program elements, including leadership, topics, themes are known, develop more detailed information. People will ask about the retreat. Anticipate questions and speak to them in all your communication, through both announcements and registration tools. People want to know the following facts about any event. In any promotion, repetition is necessary. Don't be hesitant to repeat the information again and again. Use this checklist to verify you have addressed each one of these questions in all your communication:

- What? – is happening: church family retreat, women's retreat, topic, leadership;
- When? – date and times;
- Where? – location, distance from the church, accommodations;
- How much? – cost;
- Why? – people will want to come;
- Who? – retreat is for: everybody, women, families, etc.

Announcements Tools

- Newsletters – As soon as you know a date put it in newsletter so folks can save date. Add information as you have it and emphasize why people should plan to come.
- Bulletins – Put short reminders in bulletins periodically so folks won't forget.
- Make Announcements during worship, at other group events, in Sunday school classes. Use interesting and engaging means such as skits and power point presentations. Invite people who have attended past retreats to give testimonials about the meaning of the experience for him or her.
- E-mail the membership list.
- Posters – Post them in major traffic areas such as outside the sanctuary, educational rooms, fellowship hall.
- Tee Shirts – Have the planning team wear them to make announcements.

Registration Process

Once the congregation knows about the retreat, it's time to provide them with a way to sign up. You need to have an attractive, inviting brochure, get the brochure into the hands of members, and have a plan for receiving the registration forms, money, and confirming the registration. Make the registration process as simple and uncomplicated as possible for both the registrar and congregational members.

Make use of computer programs to make an eye-catching brochure. Continue to use the graphic images you have developed and used in the announcement tools. Include in the brochure all the information you presented in the announcement, plus a retreat schedule, more details about accommodations, and a map to the retreat facility. If there is a limited number of a certain kind of accommodations such as private rooms, be sure to mention how many there are and how they will be assigned.

On the registration form within the brochure, ask for the following information about the retreat participant:

- name;
- address;
- phone and email;

- number of people coming and ages of children;
- person and phone number to contact in case of emergency;
- special dietary needs;
- whether attending the whole retreat or parts.

In case of a youth retreat, you may want to have a behavior covenant (see sample), and medical information/permission form. If you will be transporting youth to the retreat, be sure you have signed permission. Refer to the chapter on "Keeping Everyone Safe" for more information.

As soon as a registration is received, confirm the receipt of the form and be sure that each person who registers has:

- a map and directions to facility;
- the time of arrival and departure;
- a list of things they need to bring such as linens, towels, personal items, comfortable clothes, etc.

You may have included this information in the brochure, but repeat it again in the response letter.

Hand out brochures at every opportunity. You want people to find a brochure easily. Make brochures available to the target group within the church, or all groups within the church if it is an all-church retreat. Insert brochures in newsletters, display them at the rear of the sanctuary, and distribute them in person to members of the congregation or target group. Offer frequent opportunities to register, such as following worship and fellowship dinners. Encourage those who attended retreats in the past to extend personal invitations to others.

Since you are facing a deadline for giving the retreat center a participant count, you want people to sign up as soon as possible. Provide some incentives to motivate people to register early. Offer some kind of a bonus. For instance, give a t-shirt to the first ten people who register, or give away a free registration for one adult who comes with more than two children. Create an early discount for those registering before a certain date. Be sure that everyone knows there are scholarships available and how to request them.

Remember to include an adequate, non-refundable deposit to ensure retention of participants. Paying a percentage of the fee at registration, or knowing that only a percentage of the fee will be refunded, motivates members to keep the retreat a priority. Unfortunately, without a financial investment all of us are tempted to stay home or find something else to do. The retreat center will need to be paid whether people change their minds or not. Unless the church is paying the whole bill, encouraging people to follow through constitutes good financial stewardship.

How Many People Is Enough?

It is always difficult to decide when to cancel a retreat if the enrollment is low. Sometimes the retreat center minimum is not reached. Sometimes it is a financial decision if the financial plan is based on a certain number of people and that number is not reached. Sometimes there is a fear that a few people won't be "enough" to make the retreat worth doing. Congregations need to decide whether the goals of the retreat can be met even with fewer people. An advantage of the earliest possible announcement is that church members can plan ahead.

Worksheet: Timeline for Promotion and Registration

Announcements

TOOLS	PERSON RESPONSIBLE	TARGET DATE
Newsletter	_____	_____
Bulletins	_____	_____
Announcements	_____	_____
E-mail	_____	_____
Posters	_____	_____
T-shirts	_____	_____
Registration	_____	_____
Brochure	_____	_____

Sample Youth Covenant

For Youth, Adult Advisors, and Parents or Participants

This covenant is for both the YOUTH and ADULTS who attend presbytery youth events such as retreats, rally days, mission trips, youth conferences as representatives of the Presbytery of the James, etc. Seeking the guidance of the Holy Spirit, while at a Presbytery of the James youth event, I covenant to:

R: Refrain from consuming alcohol, using illegal drugs, or smoking, and Refrain from driving any vehicle for the duration of the event.

E: Enjoy the time of rest and renewal.

S: Seek to hear God's claim on my life through the opportunities provided.

P: Participate to the best of my ability in all planned activities.

E: Expect to encounter God.

C: Care for others by being a good steward of the resources provided over the course of the event including, but not limited to the food prepared, supplies provided, persons leading the event.

T: Treat the facilities with respect.

F: Friendship - take time to meet one new friend.

U: Understanding - be considerate of one another, seek to hear others.

L: Lights out - abide by the lights out policy of the event, and be in my room or cabin by that time.

_____   _____
Participant's name (please print)   Participant's signature

_____   _____
Parent/guardian's name (please print)/Parent/guardian's signature

Church _____ Date _____

The really fine print . . . (policies)

VANDALISM AND PROPERTY DAMAGE—Any person who damages or destroys property will be responsible for the cost of replacement and repair.

SMOKING—All youth events are smoke-free.

DISRUPTING EVENT ACTIVITIES—A great deal of time, effort and money go into preparing a youth event and we need your support. Disruptive behavior during assemblies, workshops or worship times or other planned activities makes it hard for everyone to get the most out of the time we have together. Participants can expect two warnings about this from any adult leader, anyone who continues to disrupt will not be invited to the next event.

PERSONAL BELONGINGS—You are responsible for your own belongings. Do not bring any items that are of great value to you.

ALCOHOL AND ILLEGAL DRUGS—Any youth or adult found in possession of illegal substances will be dismissed from the event and may be subject to arrest.

DRIVING—Vehicles driven to the event should be parked and locked. They should not be driven during the event, except in emergency.

Keeping Participants Safe

In order for retreat participants to have meaningful time, to discover a sense of belonging, and to find rest, it is essential that they feel safe—physically, spiritually, and emotionally. Encounters with God, others within community, and creation can only take place within an environment of safety and security. All participants need to know from the moment they arrive at the retreat center that they are welcomed, accepted, and protected from danger. They need to feel safe enough to explore this experience and to learn from it.

There are risks in everything we do all the time; they cannot be avoided. The very act of leaving the familiar environment of the local church to come to a retreat center for the weekend may involve anxiety about physical and emotional security. Will I be safe walking around camp at night? Will there be food I like? Will I make friends and be accepted? What will happen if I feel scared? Will I be asked to do things I am uncomfortable doing?

It is the responsibility of the Retreat Planning Committee to identify the risks—physical, emotional, and spiritual—inherent in the retreat event and to develop means for managing the risks. The risks never disappear. However, they should be anticipated and an appropriate response put in place. Without such well-developed plans, the retreat experience will not be as rich and meaningful as is possible for all retreat participants.

In many ways, forms of managed risks can actually contribute to the retreat experience. First, the concerns about entering an unfamiliar places or situations are a common denominator linking all the participants. Everyone has stepped onto a strange and new common playing field. Unlike the local church, no one owns the retreat space; everyone is a guest. Second, an environment of managed risks enables participants to step out of their "comfort zone" and to discover new things about themselves, God, and others.

Often it is during times of discomfort that we grow personally and spiritually. The opportunity to take a chance may take place during a Bible study, on a challenge course, or around the dinner table.

Hospitality practices play a role in keeping people safe. The ways in which we welcome participants into the retreat and give information about the site and the event create an environment of trust. In order to take risks—emotionally or physically—a high level of trust is essential. Hospitality is a partner with risk management practices and policies. Both should communicate a message that participants are safe and can rest in the assurance that leadership takes their need and right for safety seriously.

Managing Risks

Since there are risks in everything we do, and we cannot eliminate risks entirely from our lives, we must learn to manage them. In our personal lives we do this all the time by buying insurance, making choices about our activities and risks, and investing money for emergencies and the future.

The task of the Retreat Planning Committee is to identify possible risks and to make decisions about how to manage them. Sometimes it is appropriate to choose not to do the activity, sometimes the response includes developing policies and procedures, sometimes it means buying insurance, and sometimes the retreat center will cover the risk through contractual agreement.

Four Ways to Manage Risks

- Avoidance – not doing an activity
- Retention – including an activity because the risk is very low
- Reduction – asking how to make the activity as safe as possible through policies and procedures designed to manage the risk of the activity
- Transfer through contract – passing on the liability of the risk to someone else through such things as insurance

Kinds of Risks

Whenever you plan for a retreat, you need to identify the risks and determine ways to manage those risks. Name the areas of risk and then look at existing policies and procedures, leadership, collection of information, and behavior expectations. Use the worksheet, "Risk Management" to review areas of risk and the questions you will want to answer. Carefully reviewed each of the areas of concern in order to keep participants safe from harm, respond to emergencies, and to protect the church from litigation.

The church may have already established many of the policies and procedures that govern all church activities. Other policies and procedures related especially to taking members off church property may already be in place. If the church has no documentation in place, the Retreat Planning Committee needs to bring this to the attention of the governing board and request it to develop them.

It is always appropriate to contact the retreat center to discuss their policies and procedures for managing risk. Don't assume they have a policy of risk management in place, or that they will assume responsibility. Review the pertinent risks with them and examine their correspondence with you regarding their assumption of risk. A camp, conference, or retreat center accredited by the American Camp Association has reached the highest level of operational standards. They have in place all the policies and procedures required by this accreditation and have passed a rigorous review of all their practices by a visiting team of their peers.

Worksheet: Risk Management

Transportation

- Who will transport retreat participants?
- Have those driving provided driving records?
- Have those driving verified their auto insurance coverage and the amount of coverage they carry?
- Is the church van adequately insured and are there policies for its use? Have the drivers been trained?
- Have all vehicles passed state inspection?
- Does the church's insurance cover those driving on retreat if they are carrying youth/children? If rented vehicles are used does the church's insurance cover them?
- Have you complied with your state's booster/child safety seat requirements?

Medical Information and Policy

- Do you have medical information for minor participants attending without parents?
- Do you have permission to treat these minors in case of a medical emergency?
- Who will dispense medications and where will they be kept?
- Is someone trained in first aid and CPR available on the site?
- Will you provide participant health insurance for those attending the retreat? Does the retreat center carry health coverage for guests?
- Does the church's insurance policy cover participants when they are off the church property at a retreat?
- Has the level of medical care provided by the retreat center been clearly communicated to retreat participants?
- Have you asked participants to provide information about any medical conditions that may affect their ability to participate fully in all activities?

Behavior Expectations

- Are expectations for behavior made clear to participants before they come?
- Are policies related to alcohol, drugs and firearms stated clearly in registration materials?
- In the case of youth, will a group covenant be signed before attending?
- What does the covenant include?

Contact Information

- Do you know how to contact a next of kin for each person attending the retreat?
- Do next of kin know how to contact a family member during the retreat?
- Does the facility staff know how to find individuals in case of an emergency?

Facility Coverage and Standards

- What kinds of standards are in place at the facility to keep people safe?
- Is the facility accredited by the American Camp Association?
- How far away is the rescue squad? Is there a 911 emergency response?
- Are lifeguards required for swimming and boating? Who is responsible for verifying the certification and hiring the lifeguard?
- What kind of safety orientation is provided for participants by the facility? Do they have emergency evacuation plans in place?
- If the group will be participating in a challenge course (high or low ropes), have you asked about certification of the course and facilitators?
- Has the facility provided information about their liability coverage?

Leadership

- Does you church have policies regarding child and youth sexual abuse?
- Have you followed existing church policies regarding background checks on those who will work with children or youth?
- Have all the retreat leadership received training in abuse issues and in appropriate response to accusations of child abuse?
- Who will supervise children and youth? How will youth working with children be supervised?
- Have the credentials of any mental health professional providing direct counseling services to retreat participants been verified and has the governing body approved their presence at the retreat and their contact with retreat participants?

Liability Insurance

- Have you checked the retreat center contract to verify who is responsible for what?
- Does a liability release form exist and have all participants signed it?
- Has a tort lawyer given guidance for the liability release so that it is in accordance with your state's laws?

- Have you verified with the church/s insurance broker that the church carries liability insurance to cover events off the church property?
- Is the venue for any litigation clearly identified in the release form?[1]

Resource List

Safe Sanctuaries for Youth by Joy Thornburg Melton (Discipleship Resources, 2004).

Safe Sanctuaries: Reducing the Risk of Child Abuse in the Church by Joy Thornburg Melton (Discipleship Resources, 2003).

Safe and Secure: The Alban Guide to Protecting Your Congregation by Jeffrey Hanna (Alban Institute, 1999).

Notes

1. Many thanks to Will Evans (wevans@markelcorp.com) of Markel Corporation and Steve Coons of Covenant Presbyterian Insurance Program, Inc (steve@cpip.org) for reviewing these areas of risks and making suggestions.

Evaluating
the Retreat

Evaluation provides a way to find out whether you have achieved your purpose for the retreat. You want to know whether your goal of creating an experience of Christian community and faith formation has been reached. You also want to know what elements of the retreat made it meaningful to participants. The only way to reach that goal is to ask questions of those who attend the retreat. You want to know what they liked and what contributed to the experience; you want to know what they did not like and what interfered with the meaningfulness of the experience.

Why Evaluation Is Important

Sometimes we are reluctant to do formal evaluations because the forms we often see seem silly, we don't want to hear negative comments, or it is just too much effort in light of all the other planning and details that need attention. However, remember that people will evaluate the retreat whether you ask them to or not. They will spread the news of the retreat and urge others to attend the next year, or they will tell others that is was a waste of time and not to go another year. They will complain about the food and the speaker and the beds whether you give them a chance to say it officially or not. They will evaluate the experience by attending other retreats. In order to capture these comments, both positive and negative, evaluation needs to be a planned, intentional process, not an after thought.

It is difficult to hear negative comments about anything we have worked hard and long on. We want to hear what people liked and not what they disliked. That is human nature! However, compiling feedback about both strengths and weaknesses enables future Retreat Planning Committee to include the meaningful elements another time and work to correct weaknesses. Evaluation of the retreat will also allow you to celebrate the event and to rejoice with participants in those elements that made it meaningful.

Evaluation does not necessarily mean using a written form. Certainly you can use a written form of evaluation inviting participants to complete it individually or as a whole group. Many creative avenues of evaluation are available that lend themselves better to the retreat environment. These include a variety of interactive forms of gathering opinions from participants. See "Ten Evaluation Possibilities" at the end of this chapter for ideas about other means of evaluating the experience.

Since evaluation is an essential component of retreat planning, spend time early in the retreat planning process to decide the information you want to gather and the means of doing gathering the information. This will insure that evaluation isn't left to the last minute when you are more apt to "throw together" a couple questions on a printed form. Take the evaluation process seriously. Consider it part of your goal of providing a meaningful experience for those who attend.

What to Include in an Evaluation

Just as this book makes a distinction between administration and program elements, your evaluation process should differentiate between these two elements. Plan to ask some questions that focus on the registration and promotion process, the retreat facility (food, beds and meeting space), and hospitality. Then ask questions that invite participants to provide feedback on the program elements, including speaker, small groups, recreation, and worship. Since both elements make a contribution to the meaningfulness of the retreat experience, you will want to know that such things as other guests, dirty facilities, and poor food quality distracted from the meaningfulness of the program element and robbed participants of enjoyment of the experience.

The reason for any evaluation is to determine whether you have reached your purpose, goal, and objectives. Ask questions that seek feeling responses, as well as opinions about program activities. Begin by deciding what you want to know and then frame questions or processes that will enable you to gather that information. Be specific so participants know exactly what you are asking. Use questions that enable you to find out:

- if the retreat reached the purpose and goal the Planning Committee intended;
- what was most meaningful to participants;
- what interfered with the meaningfulness of the experience;
- what they liked and/or disliked about the facilities, accommodations, and food;
- what they thought about the registration process;

- what made them feel safe and secure, or not;
- if they would come to another retreat. Why or why not?

How to Use the Evaluation Information

Once the retreat is over, it is tempting to rest from the planning process, to put away equipment and program supplies, to thank the leaders, and to pay the final bills. However, one more task remains. You need to compile, review, and discuss the evaluations. Based on the evaluations, prepare a final report for the next Retreat Planning Committee with recommendations for elements to keep and those that need changing. Unless you are going to use the results of the evaluation, it is worthless to engage in the process in the first place.

It is tempting to look through the evaluation results immediately after the retreat when folks are packing up and the committee members are still together. A word of caution: that is a very vulnerable time for those who have spent so much time and energy on the retreat plan. Negative remarks will seem discouraging and frustrating—even hurtful. It is much better to go home and regroup individually. Plan to meet within the next week (not three weeks later when your memories will not be as fresh) to review the evaluations and discuss them.

Begin the discussion process with the purpose, goal, and objectives you developed at the very beginning of the planning process. Were the purpose, goal, and objectives reached? Was the retreat meaningful to participants? What made it meaningful? What distracted from that meaning? Discussion of these questions will enable you to evaluate whether the retreat design was faithful to your intention and whether the design was meaningful.

Next, look at what participants liked and didn't like. Differentiate between administration and program elements. If administration elements get low marks, brainstorm recommendations for the next Retreat Planning Committee that will address these concerns. Those elements are fairly easy to improve. It may mean not returning to the same retreat center, getting the date on the calendar earlier, or mailing brochures to every church member. Be specific in your recommendations to the next committee. And be sure to share facility evaluations with the site management.

Examine the feedback about each program element. Which ones did participants like and which one do they want changed? As you record and discuss the comments, be sure to keep in mind the difference between things that can be changed or adapted and things that have to do with personalities. Perhaps the speaker was long-winded and disrupted the schedule. Perhaps the crafts person was not prepared. This problem can be solved by not inviting that person another time. However, if participants wanted more time for individual reflection, an afternoon hike, or more planned recreation, then those requests can help the planning team for the next retreat.

Put all your recommendations based on evaluations, plus recommendations from workgroups about improving the planning process, into a written report. In addition to this report, prepare for the next Retreat Planning Committee a complete folder with all the paperwork from this planning process that includes:

- a planning calendar for the Retreat Planning Committee;
- a retreat schedule;
- a brochure;
- the risk management and hospitality policies and practices;
- a budget;
- contact and billing information for the retreat center and any other retreat centers you visited or contacted;
- a promotion planning calendar and samples;
- people and print resources you used or discovered.

Finally, plan some way to celebrate the experience of both the planning and the retreat. The Retreat Planning Committee has worked closely together for up to a year. Congratulation yourselves for a job well done!

Ten Evaluation Possibilities

Continuum Scales

Rank the experience, things learned, and the overall event with choices from one extreme to another. These can be done with paper and pencil ("Circle the number on the scale that indicates your feelings, with five being high and one being low"), by physical movement ("Move to that wall if your response is 'Great,' to this wall if your response is 'Terrible,' or someplace in between to indicate your experience"), or by voting ("Hold up fingers to indicate your vote, with five being high and one being low").

Expressions of Color

Place a wide variety of colored sheets of paper in the center of the group. Ask each person to choose the color that best indicates his or her response to the questions you ask. Ask questions about the experiences during the event or meeting. As the participants select a color to hold up, ask one or two to describe why they selected that color.

Graffiti Wall

Hang a large sheet of paper on the wall. Distribute a variety of large, colored markers.

Ask participants to write or draw their reflections on the experience. Encourage them to be creative, with large and colorful symbols, words, or pictures.

Musical Evaluation

Divide into groups of three or four. Ask each group to prepare a song that expresses what they gained from the experience. This type of evaluation will take some time to complete, but the result will be funny as well as informative.

Open-Ended Sentences

Distribute worksheets of sentence starters. Ask the participants to finish the sentences, telling of their experiences. Occasionally put in a funny sentence starter like, "The best thing I ate looked like . . . " or "The silliest thought or wish I had was about . . . " and so forth.

Points Count

Make a list of all the parts of the experience. Give each person fifty points. Ask them to distribute the points among the list as they choose, giving the best part all their points or distributing them (by fives or tens to help with addition) among several. After everyone votes, add up the points for each part to see what got the most points, and what didn't get any points at all. Option: Pretend the points are money. How much would they pay for each part of the experience, spending all their money?

Sentence Prayer

Ask each person to write one sentence of prayer about the experience. With a beginning sentence and an ending sentence, ask people to contribute their sentences as the body of the prayer, each in turn. Option: Ask people to group themselves and prepare five parts of the prayer: adoration, confession, supplication, intercession, and thanksgiving.

Smiley Faces

Provide each participant with a paper plate on a stick. Ask them to create a happy face on one side and a sad face on the other. Then as questions are asked, they can respond by holding up a happy face or a sad face.

Written Responses

Ask participants to write their responses, providing adequate time so that no one feels rushed. Add interest to this method by asking participants to write one comment per adhesive note, or by writing a short story telling of their experience.

Three Possible Questions

Ask three questions, allowing time for people to respond as you write their answers on newsprint, chalkboard, or dry-erase board.

- What went well?
- What did I learn?
- What needs improvement?
- What should we do differently the next time?[1]

Notes

1. Reproduced from *The Ministry of Christian Education and Formation*.